SCOTS EDUCATION LAW

By

Robert Marr LL.B, D.P.A., N.P.

and

Catherine E. Marr B.A., LL.B, Dip L.P.

W. GREEN/Sweet & Maxwell

EDINBURGH

First published 1995

© 1995
W. GREEN & SON LTD.

ISBN 0 414 01040 X

A catalogue record for this book is
available from the British Library

Typeset by Wyvern Typesetting
Printed by The Headway Press, Reading

To J.C.M.

CONTENTS

CONTENTS

APPENDICES

SCOTS EDUCATION LAW

PREFACE

If there is one subject on which almost everyone can claim to have some personal knowledge, it is education.

What we have tried to achieve in this work is to set out, in plain terms, the law relating to education in schools managed by councils in Scotland. As the book took shape, we found that we did not feel that we would be doing justice to our readers if we did not mention initiatives such as school development plans which, although they have no basis in law, now impact significantly on the life of everyone involved in the education system. We have included references to such matters where we thought it appropriate to do so in an attempt to make the whole more readily understood.

This is a book which is meant to be read by parents of children at school, teachers, administrators and even lawyers who may be coming to the subject with little previous experience in it. It does not, and indeed is not meant to, go into every nuance of statute and regulation. What it does do, we believe, is set out clearly the legal principles which apply to different situations, expanded as far as is necessary to be useful. It is written in a style which we hope reflects that goal. We have incorporated the changes in the law which will be introduced by The Local Government etc. (Scotland) Act 1994 and which will come into effect in April 1996.

Whilst the teacher's word will always be law, we trust that this book will help everyone with an interest to know what the law actually is. We believe that that can only benefit the Scottish education system, those who administer it and those who are the subject of their ministrations.

August, 1995   ROBERT MARR
                                                     CATHERINE E. MARR

TABLE OF CASES

TABLE OF STATUTES

TABLE OF STATUTORY INSTRUMENTS AND CODES

CHAPTER 1

INTRODUCTION

Children do not have to go to school, but parents have a duty 01–01
to educate them. Parents may fulfil the duty to educate their
children by other means than by sending them to school.[1]
They may choose to teach their children themselves or may
employ a private tutor to do it for them. Parents, not the education authority, then have to provide the necessary books and
materials. They may opt to send them to a private school. If
parents do decide not to send their children to school, they
are not free to teach them whatever they like!

The law requires that parents must provide for their children 01–02
of school age efficient education suitable to their age, ability
and aptitude either by causing them to attend a public school
regularly or by other means.[2] This needs a little explanation.
Sometimes the term "public school" is commonly used when
referring to a private or fee-paying school. In the sense in
which the term is used here, the type of school meant is a
school provided by a local authority which is responsible for
providing education, *i.e.* an education authority.[3] Education
authorities must secure that there is made for their area
adequate and efficient provision of school education.[4]

Education Authorities

There used to be two types of education authority—regional 01–03
councils and islands councils. Since the reorganisation of
local government in May 1996, every local authority (or

---

[1] Education (Scotland) Act 1980, s. 30.
[2] *ibid.*
[3] Education (Scotland) Act 1980, s. 135(1).
[4] Education (Scotland) Act 1980, s. 1(1).

"council") is an education authority. There used to be a requirement that the former education authorities appointed education committees to which all matters relating to education were referred. There is no such requirement on the new education authorities, although they may do so if they wish. If an education committee is appointed, there are certain rules which apply to it. At least one-half of its members must be members of the authority. Education authorities on the mainland of Scotland must appoint to the committee one representative of the Church of Scotland nominated in a manner prescribed by its General Assembly; one representative of the Roman Catholic Church nominated in a manner prescribed by its Scottish Hierarchy; and one person selected by the authority, having regard to the comparative strength of the churches and denominational bodies having duly constituted charges or places of worship in its area. In the latter case, account must be taken of the representation of the Church of Scotland and the Roman Catholic Church.

01–04   In the case of the Orkney Islands, Shetland Islands and Western Isles Councils, a representative of the Church of Scotland must be appointed, but there is no requirement for a Roman Catholic Church representative. The "other denominational" representatives are increased to two, and one of these, at least, may be from that church. Such persons have the same voting rights as elected members. There used to be a requirement to appoint two teachers employed in the authority's schools. That requirement was also removed on the reorganisation of local government. Authorities can co-opt people who are not elected members to sit on their education committees and, although no longer required to do so, they may appoint teachers in their employment to sit on their committees.

01–05   Two or more authorities may appoint a joint committee to discharge any of their functions as education authorities. This was permitted before the reorganisation of local government although it was a power which was not used. It may be that with smaller education authorities, it is more likely to be done under the new arrangements. Regional and Islands Councils were required to appoint Directors of Education. The new

Councils do not have to do so, although they may, if they choose to.[5]

Choice of Education

School age is generally between the ages of five and 16 **01–06** years. Whether a child is educated at home, at a public school, or a private school, the same age range applies.[6] Choosing to educate children at home does not mean that education authorities have nothing to do with them. They will want to be satisfied that parents are educating their children properly. They may do this by sending inspectors to visit regularly and may provide advice on what should be taught. If they are not satisfied that parents are providing the type of education which the law demands—suitable to the age, ability and aptitude of the child—then they must serve on them a notice which requires the parents to state to the authority the means they have adopted for providing education for their child. If the authority is not satisfied with the information given, it must make what is known as an "attendance order" requiring the child to go to a school named in the order.[7]

Education authorities have no supervisory role over private **01–07** schools (the law describes them as "independent" schools). That is the task of the Secretary of State for Scotland. Independent schools have to be registered by him and he has the duty to inspect them to make sure that the education which they provide is of the necessary standard.[8] There is now another type of school at which children can be educated. It is known as a "self-governing" school. In 1989, an Act of Parliament was passed which allows schools which are provided by education authorities to become self-governing. That means that the parents of pupils in attendance can vote to

[5] Local Government (Scotland) Act 1973, ss. 78, 124 and 126 as amended by the Local Government etc. (Scotland) Act 1994, s. 31, Sched. 13, para. 29 and Sched. 14.
[6] Education (Scotland) Act 1980, ss. 31–33.
[7] Education (Scotland) Act 1980, s. 37. See also Chapter 10.
[8] Education (Scotland) Act 1980, s. 98.

have the school removed from the control of the education authority. They then elect a board of management to run it for them. Before a vote can take place, the school must have a school board. The final decision on whether the school can opt out or not lies with the Secretary of State.[9]

01–08 If it is decided to educate a child at a public education authority school, a parent has some rights over how that education is provided. The law states that "education authorities shall have regard to the general principle that, so far as is compatible with the provision of suitable instruction and training and the avoidance of unreasonable public expenditure, pupils are to be educated in accordance with the wishes of their parents".[10] That is an easy thing to say. It is not so easy to put into practice when there are many, many pupils in a school and their parents may all want different things for their education. Two recent court cases helped to explain how far the rights of parents extend. One judge said: "the subsection does not provide that the wishes of the parents must in all cases prevail".[11] Another said: "It is clear that the mere fact that the decision of the respondents [the education authority] to close Stanley Green [school] was in conflict with the desire of most of the parents to keep it open goes no distance at all to establish the applicant's [parent's] case for judicial review." What is clear is that the wishes of a parent will not automatically prevail against those of an education authority.[12] What is not generally clear is when the parent's wishes will come first. The law is much more precise in the matter of children receiving religious instruction, or taking part in religious observance, when the wishes of the parent must prevail.[13]

01–09 There may be special circumstances where a child can be educated by an education authority other than in a school. The law says: "If an education authority are satisfied that by reason of any extraordinary circumstances a pupil is unable to attend a suitable educational establishment for the purpose

[9] Self-Governing Schools etc. Act 1989. See also Chapter 21.
[10] Education (Scotland) Act 1980, s. 28(1).
[11] *Keeney v. Strathclyde Regional Council*, 1986 S.L.T. 490.
[12] *Harvey v. Strathclyde Regional Council*, 1989 S.L.T. 612 (H.L.).
[13] Education (Scotland) Act 1980, s. 9.

of receiving education, they may make special arrangements for him to receive education elsewhere than at an educational establishment."[14] So, for example, if a child is suffering from a long-term illness which prevents him from attending school, an education authority might arrange for a teacher to go to the child's home. Education authorities do not have to do that, however. Whether they do or not will depend to a large degree upon the extent to which they can afford to provide such a service.

Special Circumstances

Not all families live within easy reach of schools. There are **01–10** those who live in remote areas where getting to school every day may be a difficult if not impossible task, or the conditions under which the children are living or other exceptional circumstances may prevent them from receiving the full benefit of school education. If such a family want their children to be educated at school, the education authority has a duty to cater for them. It could do that in a number of ways. It could either provide transport or a means of transport, such as bicycles. If that would not help, then it could provide board and lodging for the child so that he could go to school during the week. It could even provide for teachers to travel to the pupil and pay for the teachers' travel and board and lodging costs. None of these arrangements need be made, although they could still be, if the education authority originally made suitable arrangements for the child but, as a result of a successful placing request by the parent, the child has been placed in a different school.[15]

Education in Children's Homes

An education authority may have in its area a children's home **01–11** provided by a social work authority. Education and social

---

[14] Education (Scotland) Act 1980, s. 14.
[15] Education (Scotland) Act 1980, s. 50.

work authorities are part of the same local authority although sometimes a home may be provided by one social work authority in the area of another authority. If such a home is wholly or mainly provided to cater for children under school age, the education authority may, if they choose, provide school education in the home for the children there. Teachers in such children's homes are treated as if they are employed in a primary school.[16]

Funding of Schools

Public schools are funded by the education authority. It is their duty to pay for the upkeep of the buildings and pay the staff. The introduction of devolved school management, however, has meant that schools have a substantially greater control over their budgets than they had before. The general rule is that no fees may be charged in schools provided by an education authority, although there are exceptions to this (described below).

01–12   Books, writing materials, stationery, mathematical instruments, practice materials and other articles which are necessary to take full advantage of the education provided must be supplied to pupils who come from the area covered by the education authority free of charge.[17] An education authority may also supply pictures, records, tape-recordings, films and other materials as a means of promoting education. A library service may also be provided.[18]

01–13   In certain limited circumstances, fees may be imposed in a public school. Fees may be charged for school education in some or all of the classes in a limited number of schools under the authority's management, but only where it would not prejudice the adequate provision of free school education for the area. This might happen where, for example, one school provided by an authority gave specialist teaching in

[16] Education (Scotland) Act 1980, s. 14A.
[17] Education (Scotland) Act 1980, s. 11 and School Boards (Scotland) Act 1988, s. 9.
[18] Education (Scotland) Act 1980, s. 12.

music or dance to a standard above that which would normally be provided in school. Education authorities may award scholarships to pupils in respect of any such fees, having regard to their ability and aptitude. If a pupil attends a school provided by an authority other than that in whose area he lives, a charge may be made to the pupil's "home" authority for the education provided, whether fees are normally charged in that school or not.[19]

Schools may receive money in other ways. If a school has **01–14** a school board, it may raise funds and receive gifts of money for the school (although it may not borrow money) and spend it for the benefit of the school, having first consulted the headteacher.[20] Sometimes people want to give money or property to schools or even to increase any teacher's income. Education authorities can accept such gifts but they must administer them in accordance with the wishes and intentions of the donors and in such a way as to raise the standard of education and educational efficiency of the school.[21]

Another way in which people try to benefit all or part of a **01–15** school, or to increase the income of a teacher, is to set up a trust to help raise or distribute money. Again, the education authority must administer any money or property which it receives in accordance with the objects of the trust. Such trusts may have objects which, due to the passage of time, for example, are no longer appropriate. In this case an education authority can, with the approval of the Secretary of State, vary the trust with a view to increasing the efficiency of the school by raising the standard of education there.[22]

---

[19] Education (Scotland) Act 1980, s. 3.
[20] School Boards (Scotland) Act 1988, s. 18.
[21] Education (Scotland) Act 1980, s. 79.
[22] Education (Scotland) Act 1980, s. 80.

CHAPTER 2

NURSERY EDUCATION

02–01 Very often, a parent's first experience of the education authority will be when a child goes to nursery school.

What is a Nursery School?

02–02 A nursery school, which may be a self-contained unit, or a nursery class within a primary school, is the first rung of legally defined "school education", providing activities suitable for children who are under school age.[1] Nursery education is not, however, available to all pre-school children. Although councils have the power to provide nursery schools, they do not have a duty to do so.[2] This means that in an area where there is a restricted number of nursery places, the education authority will establish a set of criteria for admission. These vary from authority to authority depending on the facilities available. Generally, however, a number of places will be set aside for children with particular needs who may be referred to the authority by the social work department or health officials. These may include, for example, children with varying social or emotional needs who would benefit from pre-school education. In such cases, the education authority may arrange for additional professional support, such as a speech therapist, to assist the children individually.

02–03 The remainder of places available would normally then be allocated on an age basis, with the oldest pre-school children being given priority. Although nursery education may be made available on a daily basis, it may be only for a limited

---

[1] Education (Scotland) Act 1980, s. 1(5)(a)(i). See also Chapter 3 for definition of "school age".
[2] Education (Scotland) Act 1980, s. 1(2).

8

period of the day and may not parallel the primary school day. A concerned parent may obtain details of admission conditions by approaching either the nursery school or class itself, or the education authority.

How do Playgroups and Private Nurseries Differ?

It is important to distinguish nursery classes provided by edu- 02–04
cation authorities from playgroups and private nurseries. Playgroups are usually for children from the age of three and offer supervised activities for children under school age for a limited period of the day, perhaps an hour or two. The activities may be similar to those of an education authority nursery, but they are independently organised. In some areas, however, the local authority may provide facilities for them. Private nurseries are provided by private individuals or companies and charge commercial fees. They advertise the services they provide which will normally include longer hours, thus catering for the needs of working parents. Education authority provision in this area will be structured to help prepare a child for school. This is less likely to be the case in the private sector.

Qualifications of Nursery School Staff

The head teacher of a nursery school and the teacher in 02–05
charge of a nursery class within a primary school will hold a Teacher's Certificate in Primary Education, with a special qualification to act as a teacher in a nursery school or class.[3]

Administration of Nursery Schools

Nursery education is administered by the education authority 02–06
but there are some significant points to be made as far as parental involvement is concerned. As described later, legislation allows for schools to have school boards and, where

---

[3] The Schools (Scotland) Code 1956, reg. 5 as amended.

appropriate, to seek self-governing status, that is to "opt out" of education authority control.[4] The position regarding nursery school is slightly different. A nursery school cannot have a school board.[5] Similarly, it cannot become a self-governing school.[6] If, however, a primary school which has a nursery class becomes a self-governing school, then the whole school, including the nursery class, will be an opted-out school.

---

[4] See Chapters 20 and 21.
[5] School Boards (Scotland) Act 1988, ss. 1(1) and 22(2).
[6] Self-Governing Schools etc. (Scotland) Act 1989, s. 13(2).

CHAPTER 3

PRIMARY EDUCATION

What is Primary Education?

Primary education is defined as "school education of a kind 03–01 which is appropriate in the ordinary case to the requirements of pupils who have not attained the age of twelve years; and which is, in the case of a pupil with special educational needs, within the provision made for the purpose of meeting his special educational needs until he is transferred to the stage of secondary education."[1]

Which School is Appropriate?

As a child approaches primary school age, parents will give 03–02 thought to the school their child will attend. Information on local schools can be obtained at any time from the education authority. Generally, a child will be offered a place at the local school within whose catchment area he or she lives. If, however, parents want their child to go to a different school, they may write to the education authority making what is known as a "placing request". In this they specify the school which they wish their child to attend. This topic is dealt with more fully in Chapter 5.

Age of Admission

A child's primary education must begin when he or she 03–03 reaches the age of five.[2] In certain circumstances, however, a younger child may be admitted to primary school.

---

[1] Education (Scotland) Act 1980, s. 135(2).
[2] Education (Scotland) Act 1980, s. 31.

11

03–04   Every year each education authority will fix two dates, known as the "school commencement date" and the "appropriate latest date". The "school commencement date" is the date when attendance at primary school will start.[3] The "appropriate latest date" is the date on or before which a child must reach the age of five to be admitted to school on the commencement date.[4] This date must not be more than six months and seven days before the following year's commencement date.[5] In practice, this works as follows.

03–05   The new term at primary school is set to begin on August 10. Any child who is five on that date must attend. The education authority may say, however, that the appropriate latest date is March 1 the following year. So a child who will become five any time up to March 1 may be admitted to school on August 10, and this could include a child as young as four and a half years. It is important to note, however, that a child under five is not required to start school.[6] This means that parents have the choice to allow their eligible but underage child to start school, or to wait until the following year's commencement date when he or she could be as much as five and a half years.

03–06   Similarly, where an underage child does attend school, the education authority may not take any action against the parents if the child does not attend regularly.[7] On the other hand, some parents wish to have their children attend school before they are old enough to gain admission as of right. A reference to this situation is made in Chapter 5.

Age of Leaving Primary School

03–07   The age when a child leaves primary school is not precisely legally defined but would normally be 11 or 12, after completing seven full years of primary education.[8]

---

[3] Education (Scotland) Act 1980, s. 32(1).
[4] Education (Scotland) Act 1980, s. 32(4).
[5] Education (Scotland) Act 1980, s. 32(7).
[6] Education (Scotland) Act 1980, s. 32(6)(a).
[7] Education (Scotland) Act 1980, s. 32(6)(b).
[8] See further Chapter 7.

Length of School Day

When a child initially starts at primary school, it is likely that 03–08 he or she will attend only for a few hours as part of an acclimatisation process. What constitutes a full primary school day will be advised by the education authority and will be governed by the conditions of service of primary school teachers. Currently, primary teachers are contracted to have a maximum class contact time of 25 hours although it is recognised in their conditions of service that additional working time may be needed.[9]

Length of School Year

Schools have to be open for 190 days in each school year. 03–09 This requirement on education authorities does not apply if they are prevented from so doing by circumstances outwith their control. Schools may not open on Saturdays or Sundays.[10]

Curriculum

Generally, the law does not set down what children should be 03–10 taught or for how long they should be taught each subject. The exceptions are that Gaelic must be taught in Gaelic-speaking areas and religious instruction will normally also be expected to be provided.[11] Broadly, the curriculum in schools is arrived at as a result of a dialogue between education authorities and the Scottish Office Education Department. In practice, the Scottish Office regularly sends to education authorities "guidelines" on individual subjects such as reading, environmental studies, etc., which authorities are

---

[9] Scheme of Salaries and Conditions of Teaching Staff in School Education, paras. 10.8.2 and 10.8.5.

[10] The Schools General (Scotland) Regulations 1975, reg. 5, as amended.

[11] Education (Scotland) Act 1980, ss. 1(5)(a)(iii) and 8(1). See also Chapter 12 on Religious Education.

expected to follow. The extent to which they are complied with could be the subject of comment, either favourably or otherwise, in reports prepared by Her Majesty's Inspectors of Schools following inspection of individual schools.

03–11   Recently introduced has been the "5–14 development programme" for children between those ages. This initiative, which is intended to be fully operative by summer 1999, sets out areas of curriculum required to be taught in primary schools and the first two years of secondary education. In addition, it specifies the minimum time allocations for each area. These are "language", which includes reading and writing, 15 per cent; "mathematics" 15 per cent; "environmental studies", covering, for example, science, history and geography, 25 per cent; "expressive arts", including drama, music, art and physical education, 15 per cent; and "religious and moral education", 10 per cent. Under this programme a child's progress will be regularly assessed. It must be stressed, however, that these are government guidelines and could be changed.[12]

03–12   Again, while there is no legal requirement to do so, education authorities are expected to make the teaching of foreign languages available in all primary schools. The languages which are recommended are French, German, Spanish and Italian.

03–13   What would happen if education authorities did not broadly follow the guidelines is problematic. It might be that the Secretary of State would seek to invoke his powers to compel an authority to perform its duty to provide suitable and efficient education,[13] but the outcome of that would depend upon the facts of the case.

Testing

03–14   Testing of certain subjects in primary schools used to be the subject of regulations made by the Secretary of State. The

[12] See generally *The Parents' Charter in Scotland 1995*, p. 8 and Scottish Office publication *Education 5–14: A Guide for Parents*.
[13] See Chapter 18.

regulations were shortlived and it appears that they were abandoned because of the force of opposition to them. Testing is, therefore, no longer the subject of regulation but there is "advice" from the Scottish Office on how testing is expected to operate in all primary schools. There are national tests which authorities are advised to use and which form part of the "5–14 programme" referred to above. The new system is more generally acceptable to authorities and is being implemented "voluntarily" in the belief that, if it was ignored, then regulation would again surely follow. Pupils are to be tested in reading, writing and mathematics when their teacher decides that they have largely reached the test attainment targets. There are different levels of test reflecting progressive standards throughout primary education. Pupils' learning and attainment across the whole curriculum is still expected to be reported on to parents.[14]

Sex Discrimination in School

Since the introduction of the Sex Discrimination Act 1975, it **03–15** would be unlawful for an education authority to refuse a boy or girl admission to a mixed school if in the same circumstances a pupil of the other sex would be admitted. The sex of any pupil is irrelevant to admission. Similarly, it would be unlawful to refuse girls in a co-educational school admission to classes to which boys were admitted, and vice versa. This is particularly important in relation to those subjects once thought of as being designed for one sex only, for example domestic science or woodwork.[15]

Care of Pupils Generally and Playground Supervision

Under common law, an education authority has a duty of care **03–16** in respect of pupils in its charge during school hours. This

---

[14] Scottish Office Education Department Circular 12/1992.
[15] Sex Discrimination Act 1975, s. 25.

means that the authority must take reasonable steps to ensure the safety of all primary pupils.

03–17 In addition to this general duty, specific statutory obligations have been imposed. First, every local authority must take "reasonable care for the safety of pupils when under their charge", a requirement which echoes, but does not replace, the common-law duty. Secondly, the authority must ensure that at any of its primary schools attended by 50 or more pupils, there is at least one adult to supervise the children when in a playground during any break between classes.[16] In this context, an adult means a person over the age of 18 and a playground means the outdoor area provided for recreation or play at break times.[17] Although the regulation refers to a school of 50 or more pupils, it could be argued that playground supervision should be provided for less than this number in order to comply with the statutory duty to take "reasonable care for the safety of pupils". Much would depend on the circumstances pertaining at a particular school, the nature of the playground area, its security and the number of pupils.

Finally, in view of the general duty, it may be necessary to provide supervision for primary children on school premises before or after normal school hours if their early arrival or late leaving is due to the timing of official school transport.[18]

Class Sizes

03–18 The normal maximum class size for pupils in the same year in a primary school is 33, with an upper limit of 39. In some schools, classes in different years may have the same teacher. These are known as "composite classes". The maximum size of a composite class is 25.[19]

[16] The Schools (Safety and Supervision of Pupils) (Scotland) Regulations 1990, reg. 3.
[17] The Schools (Safety and Supervision of Pupils) (Scotland) Regulations 1990, reg. 2.
[18] See also para. 16–04, below.
[19] Scheme of Salaries and Conditions of Teaching Staff in School Education, paras. 10.12.1 and 10.12.2.

Staffing Ratio in Schools

The Secretary of State has issued guidance concerning the 03–19
number of teachers a school should have, based on the
number of pupils who attend. A local flexibility factor is permitted in terms of the guidance. The recommended number of
teachers ranges from one, where there are between one and
19 pupils, to 25 where there are between 632 and 658
pupils.[20]

Qualification of Staff

Before someone can teach in a public school, he or she must 03–20
be registered with the General Teaching Council for Scotland.[21] The qualifications needed to be a teacher have
changed over the years and new regulations have recently
been introduced which govern training and registration.
   No one can even be admitted to a teacher-training course 03–21
unless he satisfies the requirements for admission laid down
by the Secretary of State, is considered to be suitable by the
principal of the training establishment he wishes to attend and
is considered by its medical officer to be medically fit to teach.
The length and content of the course is determined by the
Secretary of State after consultation with the General Teaching Council for Scotland. Once a person has passed the relevant examinations, etc., he will gain a Teaching Qualification
(Primary Education), which will qualify him to teach in primary
schools or departments. He must also be recommended by
the governing body of the training establishment to the General Teaching Council for registration, having satisfied the
principal that he shows promise of success as a teacher and
that the establishment's medical officer considers that he is
medically fit to teach.[22]

[20] Scottish Education Department Circular 14, December 1978, No. 1029.
[21] Teaching Council (Scotland) Act 1965, s. 6(1).
[22] The Teachers (Education, Training and Recommendation for Registration)
(Scotland) Regulations 1993, regs. 3–6.

CHAPTER 4

SECONDARY EDUCATION

What is Secondary Education?

04–01 The law defines secondary education in the following way:
"secondary education shall be construed as a reference to
school education of a kind (i) which is appropriate in the ordinary case to the requirements of pupils who have attained that
age (twelve years) and (ii) which is, in the case of a pupil with
special educational needs, within the provision made for the
purpose of meeting his special educational needs until he
ceases to be of school age or to receive school education,
whichever is the later."[1]

Which School is Appropriate?

04–02 Children normally move up to a secondary school from one
of its "feeder" primary schools. In the case of someone
moving into a new area, information on schools will be available from the education authority, but the general principle is
that pupils will attend the school in the catchment area in
which they live. This is designated by the authority. Of course,
within certain limits, parents have the right to choose which
school their child attends. This topic is dealt with more fully
in Chapter 5.

Admission

04–03 Education authorities set the dates on which the school terms
begin for secondary schools. Unlike admission to primary

---

[1] Education (Scotland) Act 1980, s. 135(2).

school, there are no rules which govern the age a child must be before he can attend secondary school. The normal course is for children who have completed the normal seven years of primary education to graduate to secondary school at the age of 11 or 12. In the rare event that a child was sought to be admitted to a secondary school without having gone through the normal course of primary school, it would be open to the education authority to consider refusing admission on the grounds that "the education normally provided at the specified school is not suited to the age, ability or aptitude of the child."[2]

Leaving Age

A child is of school age until he reaches the age of 16 but he cannot necessarily leave school on his birthday.[3] There are formulae which apply to determine when a child can leave school. They hinge on the "summer leaving date" which is the last day of May and the "winter leaving date" which is the earlier of December 21 or the first day of the Christmas holiday period of the school. 04–04

This is how it works: (a) if a child reaches the age of 16 on or after March 1 but before May 31, he can leave on May 31; (b) if a child reaches the age of 16 after May 31, but before October 1 following, he can leave on May 31; (c) if a child reaches the age of 16 on or after October 1 but before the next winter leaving date, he cannot leave until the winter leaving date; (d) if a child reaches the age of 16 after the winter leaving date but before March 1 next, he can leave on the winter leaving date.[4] 04–05

Length of School Day

The law does not prescribe how long the school day should be. Rather, it is determined by how long teachers are required 04–06

---

[2] Education (Scotland) Act 1980, s. 28A(1). See also Chapter 5.
[3] Education (Scotland) Act 1980, s. 31.
[4] Education (Scotland) Act 1980, s. 31 (1)–(3).

to teach. Currently, teachers in secondary schools and special schools and units are only obliged to have a maximum class contact time of 23.5 and 22.5 hours respectively. The teachers' conditions of service do recognise that there may be a need to work beyond those specified times.[5]

Length of School Year

04–07 This subject is dealt with in Chapter 3. The same rules apply to secondary education.

Class Sizes

04–08 Teachers' conditions of service lay down the sizes of class they should be asked to teach. Currently, they are as follows:

Year	Normal maximum	Upper limit
S1–S2	33	39
S3	30	34
S4	30	34
S5–S6	30	

Requests to take a class larger than the normal maximum are not to be unreasonably refused. An arbitration procedure is laid down in the event of disagreement. Ratios are also laid down for teachers who work in special schools and units. These vary depending upon the nature of the special needs with which they are involved.[6]

Curriculum

04–09 Reference should be made to this heading in the preceding chapter on primary education, as the same principles apply to secondary education.

[5] Scheme of Salaries and Conditions of Service for Teaching Staff in School Education, para. 10.8.2.
[6] Scheme of Salaries and Conditions of Service for Teaching Staff in School Education, para. 10.12.

Sex Discrimination

This topic is dealt with in Chapter 3. The same rules apply to 04–10
secondary education.

Work Experience

Education authorities may make arrangements to provide 04–11
older pupils with work experience as part of their education.
This is commonly done by placing them with local employers
for a week, either to do actual work with them or to "job
shadow". Work experience can only be undertaken by pupils
between May 1 in the calendar year before the calendar year
in which they reach the upper limit of school age and the end
of the latter year. This would normally apply to pupils who are
in the fourth year of secondary education or after May 1 in the
third year.

There are, of course, laws which either prohibit or regulate 04–12
the types of employment which children may undertake. The
general rule is, however, that they do not apply to children
who are on work experience. Sometimes the law also prohibits
or regulates the employment of "young persons". In this context, a "young person" means a person over school age (16)
who has not attained the age of 18 years. The importance of
this in the context of work experience is that education authorities may not make arrangements for children under the age
of 16 to go on work placements in employment which would
be against any law prohibiting or regulating the employment
of those between 16 and 18 years old. A child who undergoes
work experience from school is covered at the place of work
which he attends by the provisions of the Health and Safety
at Work Act 1974, as if he were an employee.[7]

Allowances Payable by Education Authorities

Education authorities have the power to pay allowances to 04–13
enable persons over school age (16) to take advantage, with-

---

[7] Education (Scotland) Act 1980, ss. 123 and 125, as amended by the Self-
Governing Schools etc. (Scotland) Act 1989, Sched. 10, para. 21.

out hardship to themselves or their parents, of the facilities for school education available to them. Education authorities are not required to pay such allowances, however. They may only do so, indeed, in certain circumstances and they can only be paid to defray in whole or in part: (a) such expenses of persons attending any school as may be expedient to enable them to take full part in the activities of the school; (b) the fees and expenses payable in respect of persons attending schools at which fees are payable; (c) the maintenance of persons over school age who are attending schools. It should be noted that the school need not be in the area of the education authority. Many pupils live in the area of one authority and attend school in the area of another. Allowances may be paid in respect of a pupil attending any school in the United Kingdom.

04–14   Up until fairly recently, the Secretary of State exercised his power to make regulations laying down how this power of education authorities was to be used, but he no longer does so. Persons seeking assistance should check with their education authority as to how it exercises its power as it is likely to vary from area to area, although the Convention of Scottish Local Authorities issues advice to authorities every year as to how this power should be exercised.[8] Financial help may also be available from any local educational endowment managed by the education authority, but the opportunities are limited for that and it is unlikely that any substantial sum would be involved.

Exemption from Attendance at School

04–15   Normally, children who fail to attend school regularly will render their parents liable to prosecution because of it. It is possible, however, for a child who has been attending school to be given an exemption from further attendance. Where that has been done, a parent is freed from liability to prosecution (or any other proceeding) for failing to provide for the education of the child. Only where an education authority is satisfied

[8] Education (Scotland) Act 1980, s. 49.

that, by reason of any circumstances existing at his home, it would cause exceptional hardship to require a child over 14 years of age to attend school may they grant an exemption from attendance to enable him to give assistance at home. Conditions may be imposed as to the amount and manner of future attendance at school until the child reaches the age of 16. There is a limit to the amount of absence which can be granted at any one time, although an exemption can be renewed. Exemption cannot be given for absence beyond the next school commencement date after the date of granting of the request. So, if an exemption was granted on May 1, it could not extend beyond the start of the autumn term. Education authorities must keep a register of exemptions granted with the name of the child, the circumstances which caused the exemption to be granted and any conditions attached.[9]

Careers Service

The provision of a careers service for school children used to 04–16 be within the province of education authorities, but was assumed by the Secretary of State under the provisions of the Trade Union Reform and Employment Rights Act 1993. He now has the duty to give assistance to school children (and certain others) by collecting and providing information about people seeking, obtaining or offering employment, education and training and by offering advice and guidance. The purpose of this is to help school children to decide what employment would be suitable for them when they have finished school and what training or education they need for it.

The Secretary of State can perform his duty by making 04–17 arrangements with education authorities, other persons, or a combination of education authorities and other persons to carry out his duties for him. He may also direct education authorities to provide, or arrange to provide, some or all of the careers service. Currently, the normal way in which the Secretary of State discharges his duty is through companies formed especially for the purpose by education authorities

[9] Education (Scotland) Act 1980, s. 34. See also Chapter 10.

and local enterprise companies. If in any doubt about whom to approach, the school or education authority will be able to direct inquirers to the appropriate place.[10]

Qualification of Teachers

04–18 This matter is dealt with in Chapter 3. The only additional point to make is that the qualification awarded is a Teaching Qualification (Secondary Education) which enables someone to teach a subject or subjects in secondary schools or departments. The requirement to be registered with the General Teaching Council for Scotland also applies.

---

[10] Trade Union Reform and Employment Rights Act 1993, ss. 8–10.

CHAPTER 5

CHOICE OF SCHOOL

In general, parents accept that their child will attend the local **05–01**
school in their area. Each school has a "catchment area" determined by the education authority[1] and, in the normal course, all
children within that area will attend the designated school.

Parental Choice

Every education authority, however, in meeting its statutory **05–02**
obligation to provide education for school age pupils, must
have regard to the general principle that, within certain constraints, children are to be educated in accordance with the
wishes of their parents. The constraints, broadly stated, are
that parents' wishes will be met if they are compatible with
the provision of suitable instruction and training and avoid
unreasonable public expenditure.[2] Such parental wishes may
include educating a child at home.[3] More likely, parents'
wishes may be that a child attend a school other than that
within whose catchment area the family lives.

Provision of Information

It follows that if parents are to make an informed choice about **05–03**
the appropriate school for their child, they must have access to
information on the schools in which they are interested. Accord-

---

[1] Education (School and Placing Information) (Scotland) Regulations 1982
(S.I. 1982 No. 950), reg. 2.
[2] Education (Scotland) Act 1980, s. 28(1). *Harvey v. Strathclyde Regional
Council*, 1989 S.L.T. 612 (H.L.).
[3] See Chapter 3 *re* education of children at home.

ingly, education authorities must publish, or otherwise make available, information about their schools to inquiring parents.[4] This information may be made available at the education authority's offices, at the schools, or possibly within public libraries.[5] The information supplied should include details of the school, the number of teaching staff, the school's educational aims, details of the curriculum, arrangements for assessment of pupils, school policy on discipline, entering pupils for public examinations, arrangements for pupils with special educational needs, extra-curricular activities and more general matters such as arrangements for health care, term dates and holidays.[6]

05–04 In addition, authorities will produce guidelines on admission of children to their schools. Normally, priority will be given to children living in the catchment area of a school or, if it is a secondary school, to children coming from its local primary schools. Thereafter, preference may, for example, be given to children who have brothers or sisters already in attendance at the school. Where this is the case, the authority's admission arrangements must not discriminate between siblings belonging to its own area and siblings belonging to the area of another education authority.[7]

Denominational Schools

05–05 There are within Scotland significant numbers of denominational schools, the majority being Roman Catholic. It will clearly be of importance to many parents of a particular religious persuasion that their child attend such a school. In general, denominational schools are run by education authorities in exactly the same way as the others under their management. There are, however, matters of significance to be noted. Teachers must be

---

[4] Education (Scotland) Act 1980, s. 28B(1) and Education (School and Placing Information) (Scotland) Regulations 1982 (S.I. 1982 No. 950), reg. 9.

[5] Education (School and Placing Information) (Scotland) Regulations 1982 (S.I. 1982 No. 95), reg. 7.

[6] Education (School and Placing Information) (Scotland) Regulations 1982 (S.I. 1982 No. 95), reg. 9 and Sched. 1.

[7] Education (Scotland) Act 1980, s. 23(3A) inserted by Local Government etc. (Scotland) Act 1994, s. 32.

approved as regards their religious belief and character by representatives of the church or denominational body in whose interest the school is conducted.[8] In addition, the education authority must appoint an unpaid religious instruction supervisor, again approved as to religious belief and character, who will report to the authority on the efficiency of the religious instruction provided, and must provide facilities for the holding of religious examinations.[9] If the school has a school board, then one of the co-opted members must be a person nominated by the appropriate church or denominational body.[10]

Despite this emphasis on the denominational nature of the **05–06** school, it is not a requirement that all pupils who attend must be of that particular religious persuasion. The law requires that every school under the management of an education authority must be open to pupils of all denominations.[11] Accordingly, parents may decide that although they want their child to attend a denominational school, they do not want that child to take part in religious ceremonies or to receive religious education. This does not present a problem. It is the parents' right to make such a decision. In addition, pupils who do not take part in religious observance or who withdraw from religious instruction must not be discriminated against as regards their secular education in the school.[12]

Placing Requests

Making a request
If a parent decides that he wishes his child to attend a school **05–07** other than the local school in whose catchment area he lives, he may make a "placing request". This simply means that the parent asks for his child to be admitted to the school of his choice. The request must be made in writing to the education

---

[8] Education (Scotland) Act 1980, s. 21(2A) added by the Self-Governing Schools etc. (Scotland) Act 1989, s. 82(1), Sched. 10, para. 8(7)(*b*)–(*e*).
[9] Education (Scotland) Act 1980, s. 21(3) and (4).
[10] School Boards (Scotland) Act 1988, s. 2(7).
[11] Education (Scotland) Act 1980, s. 9.
[12] Education (Scotland) Act 1980, ss. 8(1) and 9 as amended. See also Chapter 12, Religious Education.

authority which manages the chosen school and it must specify the school to which entry is required. This is known as the "specified school". Where more than one school is referred to in the placing request, the first one mentioned will be taken to be the specified school.[13] It should be noted that a young person who is a pupil has the right to make a placing request on his own behalf. Accordingly, all references here to the parent of a child may be construed as references to the young person himself.[14]

05–08 In line with the principle that, as far as is practicable, pupils are to be educated in accordance with the wishes of their parents, an authority is under a duty to grant a placing request unless certain circumstances apply. These are as follows:

(1) If placing the child in the specified school would (a) make it necessary for the authority to employ an additional teacher; (b) give rise to significant expenditure on extending or altering the accommodation or facilities at the school; (c) be seriously detrimental to the continuity of the child's education; or (d) be likely to be seriously detrimental to order and discipline in the school or the educational wellbeing of the pupils there.

(2) If the education normally provided at the specified school is not suited to the age, ability or aptitude of the child.

(3) If the education authority have already required the child to discontinue his attendance at the specified school.

(4) If the specified school is a special school and the child does not have special educational needs requiring the education or special facilities normally provided at that school.

(5) If the specified school is a single sex school and the child is not of the sex admitted to the school.

Although an authority does not have a duty to grant the placing request if any of the above apply, it may still agree to place the child in the specified school. In effect, the authority has a certain discretion in the matter.

05–09 The authority must inform a parent in writing of its decision

---

[13] Education (Scotland) Act 1980, s. 28A(1) and (2).
[14] Education (Scotland) Act 1980, s. 28G.

on his placing request. If the request is refused, the parent must be given written reasons for the decision and be informed of his right to refer the decision to an appeal committee.[15] The right of appeal does not apply to a refusal to place a child in a nursery school or class.[16] Regulations provide that if an authority does not inform a parent in writing of its decision on a placing request, then the authority will be deemed to have refused the request. There are two different timescales where this can apply. The first is where a placing request is received by an authority on or before March 15 for entry to a school for the following autumn term. Here the relevant date by which a decision must be issued is April 30. In the case of any other request, a decision must be issued within two months of its receipt. The right of appeal would then apply.[17]

Appeal against refusal of a request
A reference to an appeal committee must be lodged within **05–10** 28 days of the receipt by the parent of the authority's decision, although the committee has power to extend that time limit if there is a good reason for the parent's delay. Where a reference has been made in respect of a child, no further reference is competent during the period of 12 months from the day on which the initial reference was lodged.[18]

The appeal committee may confirm the authority's decision **05–11** to refuse the placing request if they are satisfied that one or more of the grounds of refusal, as described in (1) to (5) above, exists and that in all the circumstances it is appropriate to do so. If the committee are not so satisfied, then they must refuse to confirm the authority's decision and require the authority to place the child in the specified school. The authority must then give effect to the placing request.

If the committee refuse to confirm a decision not to place a child in a specified school, they have the power, if the

---

[15] Education (Scotland) Act 1980, ss. 28, 28A(3) and (4).
[16] Education (Scotland) Act 1980, s. 28C(2).
[17] The Education (Placing in Schools Etc.) Deemed Decisions (Scotland) Regulations 1982, reg. 4(1).
[18] Education (Scotland) Act 1980, s. 28C(3) and (4).

authority have decided not to record the child, to require the authority to reconsider that decision.

05–12　The committee must notify their decision, and the reasons for it, in writing to the parent who made the reference and to the authority. Where they confirm the authority's decision, they must inform the parent of his right of appeal to the sheriff.[19]

05–13　An authority may receive more than one placing request relating to children at the same stage of education seeking entry to the same school. Assuming that both requests are refused, it could be that one party refers the decision to an appeal committee. If the committee find in favour of the parent, then his child must be placed by the authority in the specified school. In these circumstances, the authority must then review its decision in respect of the other child and must inform the parent of that other child in writing of its decision upon that review and the reasons for it.

If as a result of such a review, the authority continues to refuse the placing request in respect of the other child, then that decision may be referred to an appeal committee as if the decision on the review were a decision to refuse an initial placing request.[20]

05–14　If a parent is dissatisfied with the decision of the appeal committee, then he may appeal to the sheriff having jurisdiction where the specified school is situated. The appeal must be lodged with the sheriff clerk within 28 days from the date of receipt of the appeal committee's decision. The authority, but not the appeal committee, may be a party to the appeal. The matter will be dealt with in chambers rather than the open court. The sheriff may confirm the authority's decision if he is satisfied that one or more of the grounds outlined above exists and that, in all the circumstances, it is appropriate to do so. If he is not so satisfied, then he must refuse to confirm the decision and the authority will be required to give effect to the placing request.

05–15　As referred to above in respect of appeal committees, if the sheriff finds in favour of the parent and the authority have

---

[19] Education (Scotland) Act 1980, s. 28E(1)–(4).
[20] Education (Scotland) Act 1980, s. 28E(5) and (6).

refused another placing request relating to a child at the same stage of education seeking entry to the same school, then, even if an appeal committee has confirmed its decision, the authority must review the other decision and inform the other parent accordingly. If the reviewed decision is still to refuse the request, the parent has the right to refer the matter to an appeal committee. The judgment of the sheriff on an appeal is final.[21]

If a reference is made to an appeal committee and a hear- **05–16** ing is not held within two months of the receipt of the reference, or if a hearing was adjourned and a date for the resumed hearing has not been fixed within 14 days of the adjournment, then the committee will be deemed to have confirmed the decision of the authority. The right of appeal to the sheriff will then apply.[22]

The grounds for refusal of a placing request have given **05–17** rise to considerable case law, although much of it is unreported and there is some inconsistency in the decisions. It is particularly where the request has been refused because to admit a child would require the employment of an extra teacher, or extension of accommodation, that the difficulty has arisen. Should the sheriff consider the effect of granting a single appeal or the cumulative effect of granting others which may be pending? This would arise where several requests have been received for entry to the same school but the authority does not have sufficient places to grant them all.

Similarly, requests for the placement of a child who is not **05–18** yet of school age, popularly referred to as "underage placing requests", have led to litigation. Although an authority may admit under-school-age children, there is no duty to do so. When such a request is received, it should be considered by the authority in the light of the particular circumstances of the case. The child should be assessed to ascertain his emotional and intellectual development, his readiness to start school and the likely effect of early entry on the child himself and on

---

[21] Education (Scotland) Act 1980, s.28F.
[22] The Education (Placing in Schools Etc.) Deemed Decisions (Scotland) Regulations 1982, reg. 5.

other pupils at the school. As an underage child has no right to a school place, it can be argued that the refusal of an underage placing request cannot competently be referred to an appeal committee.[23]

---

[23] For further discussion see *Stair Memorial Encyclopaedia of the Laws of Scotland*, Vol. 8, para. 876, footnotes 4 and 5 and Scottish Office Education Department Circular No. 15 of 1990. For general advice on the conduct of appeal committees reference may be made to the "Code of Practice for the Constitution and Procedures of Education Appeal Committees in Scotland" prepared by the Convention of Scottish Local Authorities.

CHAPTER 6

PROVISION OF CLOTHING

Children cannot take proper advantage of school education **06–01** unless they are appropriately clothed. The law recognises this and places a duty on education authorities to make provision for children who are in attendance at any of their schools but who cannot, by reason of the inadequacy or unsuitability of their clothing, take full advantage of the education provided. The duty consists of education authorities being required to make such provision as they deem necessary to ensure that pupils are sufficiently and suitably clad during the period for which they are attending school. The duty extends to days when the school does not meet.[1] Some education authorities do this by making a payment of a fixed amount to parents. The giving of clothing vouchers for use in certain shops has also been used. It is not thought, however, that simply issuing a cheque as a matter of course for, *e.g.* £30, in itself discharges an authority's duty. In a case in 1987 this practice was challenged, but the action failed, at least partly because it was clear that the issue of a fixed grant was not the only way in which the authority concerned discharged its duty.[2]

Education authorities are under the same duty with regard **06–02** to the provision of clothing in respect of children who have reached the age of five and are waiting to begin school. The same applies to a recorded[3] child who attends a school outwith the area of the education authority in which he lives. His "home" authority is under just the same obligation to ensure that he is sufficiently and suitably clad as if he attended a school in its area.[4]

---

[1] Education (Scotland) Act 1980, s. 54(1).
[2] *Shaw v. Strathclyde Regional Council*, 1988 S.L.T. 313.
[3] *q.v.* para. 13–06 *et seq.*, below.
[4] Education (Scotland) Act 1980, s. 54(4).

06–03   The law allows education authorities to recover from parents the expense which they have incurred in providing for children in this way. However, if an authority is satisfied that the parent is unable to pay all or part of the expense incurred without financial hardship, then it need not take any action to recover its outlay.[5]

06–04   There are also circumstances where an education authority may, but need not, provide clothing for pupils such as where pupils are boarders at a school or attend a nursery school or nursery class. For some activities at school, such as physical exercise, special clothing may be desirable. Education authorities may provide this type of clothing also. In cases such as these, the normal rules regarding the recovery of the expenses of providing clothing or footwear apply.[6]

06–05   Sometimes pupils who live in the area of one authority attend school in the area of a different authority. In such cases, it is the authority which manages the school which the child attends to which parents should look for assistance (but see paragraph 06–02, above, *re* recorded children).

School Uniform

06–06   It is quite common for schools to have a recognised uniform which they encourage their pupils to wear. Indeed, if a school has a school board the headteacher must provide it with a statement of the policies of the school with regard to the wearing of uniform. Any changes in those policies must also be notified to the board.[7] No pupil is obliged to wear school uniform, although that does not mean to say that they can wear anything that they like. It is easier to approach the question from the point of view of what type of clothing would not be acceptable than from what type would be. Clearly, clothing which would be dangerous to wear in, say, a laboratory should not be allowed, although that begs the question—what happens next? Pupils cannot simply be suspended from

---

[5] Education (Scotland) Act 1980, s. 54(2).
[6] Education (Scotland) Act 1980, s. 54(3).
[7] School Boards (Scotland) Act 1988, s. 10(2)(*c*).

school. They can only be excluded on two specific grounds, which are dealt with fully in Chapter 11. It would only be if the wearing of the clothing had the effect of contravening either of those grounds that an education authority would be justified in excluding a pupil from school and it is thought that that would be difficult indeed if the only objection to the clothing was that it was not the recognised school uniform.

CHAPTER 7

TRANSPORT OF PUPILS

07–01   Before children can receive the benefit of school education, they must get to the school! Not every child is fortunate enough to live within easy reach of a school. Many, particularly in the rural parts of the country, need some kind of transport to enable them to get there. Both parents[1] and education authorities have responsibilities when it comes to making sure that children actually arrive at school.

07–02   Education authorities have certain responsibilities for the transport of children to school. They have a general duty to make such arrangements as they consider necessary for the provision of any of the following facilities in respect of pupils attending schools or other educational establishments: (a) for their conveyance without charge for the whole or part of the journey between their homes and the schools or other educational establishments which they are attending; (b) for making bicycles or other suitable means of transport available to the pupils, or to their parents for the use of the pupils, upon such terms and conditions as may be arranged, or for paying money allowances in lieu thereof; (c) for paying the whole or any part, as the authority thinks fit, of their reasonable travelling expenses.

07–03   More than one of the facilities mentioned in (a) to (c) may be made available to the same child. For example, a bicycle may be provided for a child to ride to the nearest stop for the school bus which he can then take to the school.[2] Under-standing the duty on education authorities to "make such transport arrangements as they consider necessary" is a somewhat convoluted process. The starting point is that children must attend school unless they have a reasonable

---

[1] *Devon County Council v. George* [1988] W.L.R. 1386 (H.L.).
[2] Education (Scotland) Act 1980, s. 51(1).

excuse.[3] If they do not have a reasonable excuse for not attending, then their parents can ultimately be prosecuted and/or the child referred to the children's panel.[4] As indicated, however, neither of these things can happen if a reasonable excuse can be established for the child not attending school. One reasonable excuse is that there is: "within walking distance of the child's home measured by the nearest available route no public or other school the managers of which are willing to receive the child and to provide him with free education" and the education authority has either made no travel arrangements for him, or the arrangements are such as to require him to walk: (a) more than two miles if he is under eight years old; or (b) more than three miles if he is over eight and under 16.[5] Two examples will hopefully make this clear.

Example one
If a child aged seven lives in the catchment area of a school **07–04** four miles away and there is no other school where he can get free education within two miles of his home, then the education authority will be certain to provide transport for him.

Example two
If a child aged 14 lives in the catchment area of a school **07–05** two miles away, then the education authority need not provide transport for him.

Catchment Areas/Placing Requests

The two examples given above both refer to "catchment **07–06** areas". Education authorities divide up their area into sections (commonly known as "catchment areas") based on the primary and secondary schools which they have. Children who live in a particular catchment area are expected to attend the school for their area and it is on that basis that authorities make their transport arrangements. Parents can, however,

---

[3] Education (Scotland) Act 1980, s. 35(1).
[4] Social Work (Scotland) Act 1968, s. 32(2)(*f*).
[5] Education (Scotland) Act 1980, s. 42(1) and (4).

make a placing request for their child to attend a different school, which the authority must generally grant, although in certain circumstances it can legitimately refuse. If a placing request is granted, there is no obligation on the authority to provide transport for the child to get to his chosen school, so long as it has offered him a place at another school and transport to get there, if needed, in accordance with the normal rules. If the authority wishes to provide transport for such a child, however, it may do so.[6]

Exceptional Cases

07–07   For some children, it is necessary for exceptional arrangements to be made to enable them to get the full benefit of school education. There are a number of reasons for this. The child's home may be in a remote part of the country; the conditions under which he is living, or other exceptional circumstances, may prevent him from taking full advantage of his schooling; or the school which he would normally be expected to attend may not be able to provide education which is best suited to his age, ability and aptitude. In such cases the education authority must make arrangements, either permanent or temporary, for the child to attend an appropriate school best suited to his needs. Before making any such arrangements, his parents must be consulted. Thereafter, the expenses of travelling to the school would be payable, or other travelling facilities would be provided.[7] It should be noted that the school decided upon under these arrangements can be anywhere in the United Kingdom, not just in Scotland.[8] Again, if a child requiring exceptional arrangements to be made attends a school as a result of a placing request, *i.e.* a school not chosen by the education authority,

---

[6] Education (Scotland) Act 1980, s. 42(1A). See Chapter 5 on placing requests.
[7] Education (Scotland) Act 1980, s. 50(1) and (2).
[8] Education (Scotland) Act 1980, s. 50 as amended by the Self-Governing Schools etc. (Scotland) Act 1989, Sched. 10, para. 8(10).

the authority does not have to pay travelling expenses, although it may do so if it wishes.[9]

Odd though it might appear at first, there is provision for   07–08
the Secretary of State, by issuing regulations, to "deem" particular classes of children, for the purpose of their education, as belonging to an authority other than that in whose area they live. So far no such regulations have been made. It is clear, however, that if this provision were to be given effect in the future, the duty to make arrangements for pupils in the exceptional circumstances outlined above would not apply to the authority to which the children were deemed to belong.[10]

Privilege Lifts

Where an authority provides transport for children, it often   07–09
happens that there are spare places in the bus or taxi used. In such a case, the spare places must be offered, without charge, to children selected by the authority who would not otherwise be entitled to the transport. This kind of arrangement is commonly known as a "privilege lift". It should be borne in mind, however, that should another child come along who is entitled to free transport, then the authority can require the child who has the privilege lift to give up his place. Before doing so, it should give as much notice as it reasonably can of the change whilst honouring any commitments given to parents about the length of time for which transport would be available. There may also be an obligation to consult affected parents before withdrawing privilege lifts.[11]

Impact of Local Government Reorganisation

The reorganisation of local government had an impact on the   07–10
transport arrangements which the former education authorit-

---

[9] Education (Scotland) Act 1980, s. 50(1) and (3).
[10] Education (Scotland) Act 1980, s. 50(4) and s. 23(3).
[11] Education (Scotland) Act 1980, s. 51(2). See also "Complaint against Newham LBC"; *Education Law Monitor*, Feb. 1995.

ies had made, as most of the geographical areas of the former authorities were altered when the new ones came into being. The Local Government etc. (Scotland) Act 1994, which brought about the changes, recognised that the alteration of areas might cause some difficulties, and contained provisions to try to ease them. For example, education authorities are given the power to agree that pupils belonging to area "A" may be educated at a school belonging to authority "B".[12] In a case such as this, the duty to provide transport would lie, subject to the normal rules about walking distance, etc., with the authority in whose area the child lived and not with the authority whose school he attended. Similarly, where a child attended a school in his catchment area before the new authorities were created and subsequently found that school to be in the area of an authority other than the one in which he lived, it would be his "home" authority which was required to provide transport for him.[13]

The power of an authority to provide transport in cases where a placing request has been accepted in respect of a child applies also where the authority proposes to place him in a school managed by another education authority in accordance with the arrangements which existed before the new authorities were created, or as agreed between the two after they came into being.[14]

Safety of Transport

07–11 Having discussed the question of entitlement to transport, there are other matters which may be of concern regarding the way in which transport is provided. Sometimes parents have concerns, where transport is provided by bus, minibus or taxi, about such things as children sharing seats, whether or not seatbelts and escorts are available and the suitability

---

[12] Education (Scotland) Act 1980, s. 23(1A) inserted by the Local Government etc. (Scotland) Act 1994, s. 32.
[13] Education (Scotland) Act 1980, s. 51(2AD) inserted by the Local Government etc. (Scotland) Act 1994, s. 145.
[14] Education (Scotland) Act 1980, s. 50(3) and 51(2A) as amended.

of the driver. Authorities should ensure that vehicles are not overcrowded, whether they provide the transport themselves or through a contractor. It is quite legal, however, for children under the age of 14 to travel three to a seat meant for two, in a vehicle designed to carry more than eight passengers, although authorities may choose not to permit that.[15]

There are no special rules about the provision of seatbelts **07–12** in vehicles carrying schoolchildren. There is a lot of concern about children being driven in minibuses or buses which do not have seatbelts fitted, although such vehicles are generally acknowledged to be safer than cars. What authorities can do is either to provide only vehicles which have seatbelts fitted or to specify in their contracts that only such vehicles may be used, although what might be described as full-size buses do not offer that facility.

Danger to pupils does not only arise from road users. Their **07–13** fellow passengers may also prove disruptive. Escorts have been provided on buses in some instances to ensure that good order is maintained. It is not the general practice, however, and it is open to argument whether or not an authority would be in breach of its general duty of care if it did not choose to provide them. A court case might well turn on whether or not there had been any history of trouble on a particular route prior to the incident in question. When providing transport for children with special educational needs, however, an authority might be held to be negligent if an accident occurred whilst transporting pupils which might have been prevented by the presence of an escort, simply because of the increased level of dependency of the children concerned. Again, any court case would be likely to be decided on its particular facts.

Concern might also be felt about the suitability of a driver **07–14** to be left in sole contact with a child whilst taking him to or from school. There is a general system for checking the criminal records of employees of an authority who have substantial access to children and this should ensure that people who have a relevant criminal conviction are not placed in a position

---

[15] The Public Service Vehicles (Carrying Capacity) Regulations 1984 (S.I. 1984 No. 1406).

of trust, such as that of a driver. The system can also be used for privately-employed drivers. There are safeguards to ensure that any information received from the police is not passed on to the person's employer, who would simply be told that the individual could not undertake the work.[16]

Hostels

07–15 In some cases, such as in the islands, it may be impossible for transport to be arranged to get pupils to school and home again without, *e.g.* an undue length of time being spent simply travelling. To cater for such situations, education authorities have the power to provide and maintain hostels for pupils attending educational establishments in their areas.[17]

---

[16] Scottish Education Department Circular no. 5/1989.
[17] Education (Scotland) Act 1980, s. 13.

CHAPTER 8

MEALS AT SCHOOL

An education authority has a discretion to provide milk, meals, **08–01** or other refreshment for pupils at its schools and it may do this either on the school premises or elsewhere.[1] If an authority does decide to provide food or other refreshment for pupils, it must charge for this[2] and must charge every pupil the same price for the same quantity of the same thing.[3] There is, however, an exception for pupils whose parents are in receipt of income support, when the authority has a duty to provide a free midday meal.[4]

In the main, school meals are widely available but it is up **08–02** to the parents whose children qualify for free school meals to bring this to the attention of the school as the authority will be unaware of an individual child's circumstances. The authority will normally introduce procedures for payment of meals in such a way as to avoid, as far as possible, any identification of children receiving free meals.

For those children who prefer to bring their own food to **08–03** school, the authority must provide what it considers to be appropriate facilities for them to eat lunch.[5] In the majority of cases, individual schools will determine what are appropriate facilities for eating packed lunches.

When children remain at school for their lunch, the authority **08–04** has a duty to ensure their safety and supervision, although how this is organised may vary from school to school. Any

---

[1] Education (Scotland) Act 1980, s. 53(1)(*a*) as amended by s. 77(1)(*b*) of the Social Security Act 1986.
[2] Education (Scotland) Act 1980, s. 53(2).
[3] Education (Scotland) Act 1980, s. 53(2), inserted by s. 77(2) of the Social Security Act 1986.
[4] Education (Scotland) Act 1980, s. 53(3), inserted by s. 77(2) of the Social Security Act 1986.
[5] Education (Scotland) Act 1980, s. 53(1)(*b*).

supervision by teachers will be on a voluntary basis as such duties do not form part of their conditions of employment. The school would be expected to take reasonable steps to ensure that children could not leave the school premises at lunchtime without their parents' permission. If, however, parents have agreed that their child may leave the school during the lunch break, then the parents become responsible for their safety.[6]

---

[6] See also Chapter 16.

CHAPTER 9

KEEPING OF RECORDS ON PUPILS

Once a child has been admitted to a school, the education 09–01
authority must keep records about him covering a number of
matters. Whilst the records are kept by the authority, access
to them may be obtained free of charge, in certain circumstances, by the pupil (if over 16 years of age) or his parent.[1]

Registers

It is clear that schools need to know who the pupils in attend- 09–02
ance are. They are required to keep what is known as a register of admission and withdrawal. This shows when each pupil
was admitted or re-admitted to the school and his full name
and date of birth. If he has been withdrawn from school, the
date and reason for his withdrawal must be shown also.[2]

Another important record which must be kept is the attend- 09–03
ance register. Every school with day-pupils must have one.
The head teacher is responsible for its upkeep. In it must be
recorded the absence of any pupil at the school for either or
both of the morning and afternoon sessions each day.[3] This
is of particular importance in the prosecution of parents for a
child's non-attendance at school, as the production in court
of a certificate by the headteacher giving particulars of attendance of a pupil is, if properly made out, sufficient evidence of
what it contains unless evidence is led to the contrary.[4]

---

[1] The Schools General (Scotland) Regulations 1975 (S.I. 1975 No. 1135) and
the School Pupil Records (Scotland) Regulations 1990 (S.I. 1990 No. 1551),
reg. 4.
[2] The School Pupil Records (Scotland) Regulations 1990, Sched. 1, paras.
1 and 2.
[3] The School Pupil Records (Scotland) Regulations 1990, Sched. 1, para. 5.
[4] Education (Scotland) Act 1980, s. 86(c).

09–04   Sometimes when a child is absent from school he can, for the purposes of the register, be deemed to be present. This happens where the education authority has approved his absence and he complies with any condition regarding it attached by the authority. This rule does not apply to absence due to sickness. Where exemption from attendance has been granted the child is still to be marked as absent; likewise where a child has been temporarily excluded from school![5]

09–05   Boarding schools do not keep attendance registers in the same way as day schools. However, they do have to keep a register showing the date on which a pupil came into residence, the date residence ceased and the dates of, and reasons for, any period of absence from the normal activities of the school. Residence in a hostel while attending a school does not count as being in a boarding school and the school's normal attendance register would be used for such children.[6]

09–06   All of these registers must be preserved for five years after the end of the school year in respect of which they have been kept.[7]

Pupil's Progress Records

09–07 Perhaps the most important record which an authority has to keep on children attending its schools is the pupil's progress record. Each record must be checked and adjusted as necessary at least once a year and also if the child is transferred to another school. The following information must be kept in this record:

(a)   The pupil's full name and address, date of birth, position in his family and his parent's name and address, occupation and, where appropriate, place of work.

(b)   The name and address of any person other than the parent who may be notified in the case of any emergency affecting the pupil.

(c)   Any schools attended by the pupil, with dates of admis-

---

[5] Schools General (Scotland) Regulations 1975, Sched. 1, para. 5(2).
[6] Schools General (Scotland) Regulations 1975, Sched. 1, para. 6.
[7] Schools General (Scotland) Regulations 1975, Sched. 1, para. 7.

sion and leaving and the designation of the class from which he left.

(d) The results, with dates, of any objective or diagnostic tests administered to the pupil.

(e) A note of any factors adversely affecting the pupil's educational capacity or attainment.

(f) The pupil's health record.

(g) Where appropriate, information about the pupil's emotional and social development.

(h) The pupil's educational progress during each annual stage of school education.

(i) Where the pupil is in attendance at a secondary school, information about any positions of responsibility held by him in the school or, where appropriate, in any organisation.

If a pupil's progress record indicates that he has been, at some **09–08** point, excluded from school, then it must also indicate the decision of any appeal committee or sheriff following on it. As soon as is practicable after an entry to that effect has been made in the record, the parent must be informed of its terms. If the pupil is aged 16 years or over, then he should be so informed instead. In such a case it is thought that it is good practice for the school to tell both parent and pupil. If an appeal committee or a sheriff has annulled a decision to exclude a pupil, then any mention of exclusion in a record may not be disclosed.[8]

Pupils With Special Educational Needs

Particular records must be kept for pupils with special educa- **09–09** tional needs. This topic is dealt with in Chapter 13.

Access to Information

There are some kinds of information about pupils to which **09–10** access can be obtained. The rules governing this are very complicated. The type of information to which they apply is personal information which: (a) is held in a pupil's progress record kept

---

[8] Schools General (Scotland) Regulations 1975, reg. 10.

47

in accordance with the Schools General (Scotland) Regulations 1975 or in any other record kept by an education authority for the purpose of the discharge, in relation to school education, of their functions under section 1 of the Education (Scotland) Act 1980[9]; and (b) relates to a person who receives, or has received, school education provided by the authority. It is important to note that the 1975 Regulations do not apply to information recorded before they came into force except where it is required to make information recorded thereafter understandable! They came into effect on October 1, 1990.[10]

09–11 "Personal information" is defined as "information which relates to a living individual who can be identified from that information (or from that and any other information in the possession of the authority keeping the record) and includes any expression of opinion about the individual." Only a small category of persons can gain access to this information. They are:

(a) The pupil, where (i) he is not less than 16 years of age; or (ii) he is less than 16 years of age, and a parent of the pupil consents to his request.

(b) A parent of the pupil where the pupil is less than 18 years of age.

(c) A parent of the pupil, where the pupil is not less than 18 years of age but is not in the opinion of the education authority capable of understanding the relevant information in respect of which access or rectification is sought.[11]

09–12 The general rule is that if any of these persons ask in writing for information relating to a pupil, then it must be given free of charge. The authority may decide how the information is given. For example, copies of the information may be sent or simply made available for inspection at the school or council

---

[9] Section 1 sets out the general duty of authorities to provide school education including education for children with special educational needs.

[10] The School Pupil Records (Scotland) Regulations 1990, reg. 3.

[11] The School Pupil Records (Scotland) Regulations 1990, reg. 2 (the term parent "includes guardian and any person who is liable to maintain or has the actual custody of a child or young person". If the authority thinks that the pupil is not capable of understanding the information, then the term "parent" includes anyone legally entitled to administer his affairs or who has assumed actual responsibility for him.

office. The authority must satisfy itself that the person asking for the information is one of those entitled to receive it. It may also need to ask the person for information to prove that he is who he says he is.[12]

Not all information held by an authority must be disclosed. **09–13** Access to the following types of information cannot be required:

(a) Information kept, and intended to be kept, by an employee of the education authority solely for his own use.

(b) Information contained in a copy of a reference given by the education authority or one of its employees to a person who has requested it in connection with an application by a pupil for employment, education or training.

(c) Information contained in a record of needs kept under section 60 of the Education (Scotland) Act 1980.

(d) Information in respect of which a claim to confidentiality between client and professional legal adviser could be maintained in legal proceedings.

(e) Information which has been supplied to the education authority by a person, other than an employee of the education authority, subject to a legal obligation that it shall not be disclosed.

(f) Where disclosure of the information would in the opinion of the education authority be likely to cause serious harm to the physical or the mental health of the pupil or any other person (in this case the opinion of the Health Board or relevant health professional rules—see below).

(g) Where disclosure of the information would in the opinion of the education authority be likely to prejudice the prevention or detection of crime or the apprehension or prosecution of offenders (in this case, the opinion of the reporter to the children's panel rules—see below).

Where the records of an authority contain information as to **09–14** the physical or mental health of a pupil which is believed to originate from or have been supplied by, or on behalf of, a health professional then special rules apply. Access is not

---

[12] The School Pupil Records (Scotland) Regulations 1990, reg. 4(1) and (2).

required to be given if disclosure would have the effect referred to in (f) above. To determine this, the authority must consult either the health board, or the appropriate health professional if he was not employed by a health board, within 14 days of the request being received. The authority must abide by the opinion which it receives from the health professional on whether or not disclosure of information may be made.

09–15 Similarly, where the records of an authority contain information which is believed to have originated from or have been supplied by, or on behalf of, a reporter to a children's panel, the authority must seek the reporter's opinion within 14 days of receipt of the request. If the reporter advises that disclosure would have any of the effects detailed in (f) and (g) above, then access cannot be required to be given.

09–16 In both cases, if access would disclose the identity of another living person (apart from the pupil or the person who is requesting access) as someone to whom the information applies, or as the source of the information, or as someone whose identity could be worked out from the information and the likely knowledge of the person seeking it, then access cannot be required unless the other person consents.[13] Indeed, following on from this, there is a general rule that information relating to third parties, as detailed in the previous sentence, cannot be disclosed without their consent. Again, however, there are exceptions. If the third party is an employee of the education authority in pursuance of its functions relating to education and he is mentioned in his capacity as such, then his consent is not needed. Similarly, as regards information as to the physical or mental health of a pupil, if the third party is a health professional who has been involved in the care of the pupil and is mentioned in that capacity, then his consent is not required.[14]

09–17 As with so many of the regulations governing access to information, there are special rules relating to information about examinations and continuous assessment. The time limits for reply vary depending upon, for example, when results are announced.[15]

---

[13] The School Pupil Records (Scotland) Regulations 1990, regs. 5, 7 and 8.
[14] The School Pupil Records (Scotland) Regulations 1990, reg. 6.
[15] The School Pupil Records (Scotland) Regulations 1990, reg. 9.

The general rule is that the information must be supplied **09–18** within 40 days of receiving the request for it. If further details are needed to help decide if the person making the request is entitled to receive the information, then the period runs from the date on which the authority receives those details. There are, however, exceptions to this rule. If reference has to be made to a health board, appropriate health professional, or reporter to the children's panel, then the response to the request has to be made within 20 days of receiving a reply or within the 40 days, if later.

Where the consent of a third person is necessary before **09–19** access can be given, this consent must be sought within 14 days of receipt of the request. If such consent is received, then access to the information must be given within 20 days of its receipt or within 40 days if later. Notwithstanding this, the authority must give access to as much of the information as is possible without disclosing the third party's identity, for example by omitting names or other particulars. This limited access should be provided within the normal time limit. There are no time limits within which a health board, appropriate health professional, reporter or third party need reply.[16]

Inaccurate Information

A person has the right to have inaccurate information rectified **09–20** or erased. If there is a dispute over whether information is inaccurate, the authority must put a written note of the person's view with the information and give him a copy of the note free of charge. It must also give a copy of any information which has been rectified, also free of charge.[17]

Review of Decisions

If an authority refuses to give access to information or to rectify **09–21** or erase information, then the person making the request may,

---

[16] The School Pupil Records (Scotland) Regulations 1990, regs. 4 and 6(5).
[17] The School Pupil Records (Scotland) Regulations 1990, reg. 10.

within 28 days, appeal against the decision. The appeal must be heard by a sub-committee of the education committee, none of the members of which took part in the original decision. The appeal may be made either in person or in writing.[18]

Data Protection

09–22 It is commonplace nowadays for information to be kept, not on sheets of paper in files, but on computer. Different rules apply, in that event, to those outlined above. Individuals still have a right of access to the personal information which someone holds about them and can obtain a copy of that information. Requests for access must be made in writing to the person holding the information. Authorities must have a particular address which they must give to the Data Protection Registrar, to which such inquiries must be sent. It may be, therefore, that requests need to be made, *e.g.*, to the head-quarters of the authority, rather than the school itself.

09–23 A fee may be charged for the service, but it is not compuls-ory that this be done. If payable it should be sent with the request but, even if it is not, that does not stop the time limit for reply (40 days) from running. It must, however, be paid before the information is released. The 40 days do not start where: (a) information is required to identify the person seek-ing access; (b) information is required to locate the informa-tion; or (c) consent is required from another individual. Any information given must be in a form which is understandable by the person seeking it. All of the personal data held must be given and not edited in any way. Proof of identity of the person seeking the information may be required. If another individual can be identified from the data which would be dis-closed, then the consent of the other person has first to be obtained.

09–24 Information about examinations is subject to special rules. The time limits for disclosure are either the end of five months or the end of 40 days from the day on which the examination

---

[18] The School Pupil Records (Scotland) Regulations 1990, reg. 11.

results are announced. If the 40 days are exceeded, then all the information held at the date of the request and up to the date of reply must be given. This may involve giving information in original and updated forms. The right of access may be exercised by pupils themselves if they are capable of understanding the nature of what they are doing. In such a case, data should only be given to the pupil's parent as a result of a request if the pupil has authorised it.

If a pupil suffers damage because of data held concerning **09–25** him which is not correct, he may claim compensation from the authority. The damage must have been suffered after May 10, 1986! A pupil may also ask the Data Protection Registrar, sheriff court, or Court of Session to order correction or erasure of data held about him if it is inaccurate as to fact as opposed to opinion. The Data Protection Registrar has published a series of simple guidelines on data protection generally which can be obtained from his office at Springfield House, Water Lane, Wilmslow, Cheshire SK9 5AX.

CHAPTER 10

ATTENDANCE AT SCHOOL

10–01 All children of school age, that is between the ages of five and 16,[1] must attend school regularly unless they have a reasonable excuse, such as illness, for being absent. So if a child misses school occasionally and the absence is explained, this will generally be accepted. If, however, a child is frequently absent without good reason, then the education authority can take action to ensure regular attendance.[2] In fact, the failure to attend school regularly may give rise to a number of consequences.

Penalties for Non-attendance

Prosecution of the parent
10–02 The law states[3] that where a child of school age who has attended school once fails to attend his school regularly without reasonable excuse, his parent is guilty of an offence. This reflects the fact that although it is the duty of the education authority to provide education for children,[4] it is a parent's duty to ensure that his child receives that education, generally by making sure that the child attends school regularly.[5]

10–03 If, however, a parent wishes to educate a child who has previously attended school at home and the authority has agreed to this, then non-attendance at school will not constitute an offence.[6] If the authority considers that such an offence has been committed, it must serve on the parent a notice

---

[1] See Chapters 3 and 4 for definition of school age children.
[2] Education (Scotland) Act 1980, ss. 37 and 38.
[3] Education (Scotland) Act 1980, s. 35(1).
[4] Education (Scotland) Act 1980, s. 1(1).
[5] Education (Scotland) Act 1980, s. 30.
[6] Education (Scotland) Act 1980, s. 35(1).

asking him to appear before the authority to explain the child's absence.[7] The parent must be seen by the authority not less than 48 hours and not more than seven days after the service of the notice and he will be told where he is to go for this meeting.

In practice, the parent may be seen by a special sub- **10–04** committee of the education authority or by an official, the headteacher, or in some cases the school board. This will vary from authority to authority. If the parent cannot satisfy the authority that there was a reasonable excuse for his child's absence, then the authority may decide to prosecute the parent immediately. Alternatively, it may give the parent a warning and postpone the decision whether to prosecute for a period of up to six weeks.[8] If during these six weeks the child resumes regular attendance at school, then it is unlikely that a prosecution will go ahead.

If criminal proceedings are brought, these may be at the **10–05** instance of the procurator fiscal to whom the authority has referred the case, or of another person authorised by the authority to institute proceedings. This is likely to be an education-authority solicitor. The case would be brought in either the district or the sheriff court.[9] If convicted, the parent will be liable to a fine or a term of imprisonment, or both.[10]

Reference to the children's panel

Whether or not the parent is convicted, if the court before **10–06** which a prosecution is brought is satisfied that the child has failed to attend school without reasonable cause, then it can direct that the case be referred to the reporter to the local children's panel. If the court takes this step, it also certifies that the failure to attend school is established for the purpose of any proceedings before the children's hearing.[11] In other words, when the case comes before the panel the parent cannot argue that the grounds for referral do not exist.

[7] Education (Scotland) Act 1980, s. 36(1).
[8] Education (Scotland) Act 1980, s. 36(1).
[9] Education (Scotland) Act 1980, s. 43(2).
[10] Education (Scotland) Act 1980, s. 43(1).
[11] Education (Scotland) Act 1980, s. 44(1).

10–07   If the education authority has decided to start criminal proceedings then, notwithstanding the court's power to refer the
child to the reporter, it may decide to make such a reference
itself.[12] This would then proceed in the normal way pending
the court hearing. In such a case, the parent could argue that
there were no grounds for the referral and the children's panel
would then have to refer the matter to the sheriff, in order that
he might rule on the matter, before it could take any further
action.

Attendance order
10–08   If the decision whether or not to prosecute the parent is postponed then, if the child is still of school age, the authority may
make an attendance order in respect of the child. This means
that the parent is required to ensure that his child attends a
particular school which will be named in the attendance order.
This will either be the school at which he was previously a
pupil or, if the child has changed address, the new local
school.[13] As mentioned above, if the parent complies with the
terms of the attendance order, then six weeks later, when the
decision whether to prosecute is reviewed, it is unlikely that
criminal proceedings will be started.
10–09   There are other circumstances where an attendance order
may be made. First, where a parent has chosen, with the
agreement of the education authority, to educate his child at
home, but the authority is not satisfied that the parent is providing adequate education, then the authority must serve a
notice on the parent requiring him to appear before the
authority to provide information about the way in which he is
educating the child. Alternatively, the parent can send this
information to the authority in writing.[14] If, as a result of this, the
parent cannot satisfy the authority that he is providing proper
education for his child, nor that there is a reasonable excuse
for his failure to do so, then an attendance order may be made
requiring the child to attend school.[15] Secondly, where a

---

[12] Education (Scotland) Act 1980, s. 36(3).
[13] Education (Scotland) Act 1980, s. 36(2).
[14] Education (Scotland) Act 1980, s. 37(1).
[15] Education (Scotland) Act 1980, s. 37(2).

parent is prosecuted in respect of his child's failure to attend school, as referred to above, and the court is satisfied that there was no reasonable excuse for the absence, then the court may make an attendance order.[16]

General Provisions Regarding Attendance Orders

As already explained, an attendance order is an order in writ- **10–10** ing, requiring the parent to make sure that his child regularly attends a specified school, not necessarily an education authority school, which must be prepared to take the child.[17] Where an order is being made by the authority rather than the court, either because of irregular attendance or a failure by the parent to provide appropriate education at home, then the authority must first consider any view of the parent as to which school he wants his child to attend.[18] A copy of the order must be served on the parent, and thereafter it is the parent's duty to see that the child regularly goes to school.[19] If, however, the parent does not agree with the making of the attendance order, he has the right to appeal to the local sheriff. He must do this within 14 days of the date on which a copy of the order was served on him. The sheriff may confirm the order, in which case the parent must comply with it, or he may vary the terms of the order, for example by changing the school which the child is to attend. He may also annul the order, in which case it will have no effect. The decision of the sheriff is final and there is no further appeal.[20]

When an attendance order is in force, the education author- **10–11** ity may serve another notice on the parent telling him that it intends to vary the original order by specifying a different school which the child must now attend.[21] Again the parent has 14 days to write to the authority outlining any objections he has to the amendment. The authority must consider such

---

[16] Education (Scotland) Act 1980, s. 44(2).
[17] Education (Scotland) Act 1980, s. 38(1).
[18] Education (Scotland) Act 1980, s. 38(3).
[19] Education (Scotland) Act 1980, s. 38(4).
[20] Education (Scotland) Act 1980, s. 38(5).
[21] Education (Scotland) Act 1980, s. 39(1) and (2).

objections but may then amend the order as proposed. As with the original order, a copy must be served upon the parent, who has the right of appeal to the sheriff.[22]

10–12   A parent also has rights as regards amending an existing attendance order. First, he may apply to the authority asking that another school be substituted for that named in the order. Or he may request that the order be revoked because arrangements have been made for the child to receive appropriate education at a school other than the one named in the order. In either case, the authority must agree with the request unless it believes that the proposed change of school is unreasonable or not in the child's interests, or that the arrangements for the child's education at the "new" school are unsatisfactory. If the authority does not reach a decision on the parent's application within one month, or if it refuses to agree to the parent's request, then the parent may appeal to the sheriff.[23]

10–13   Once made, an attendance order remains in force for as long as the child is of school age unless it is annulled by the sheriff or revoked by the education authority.[24] When it is in force and a copy has been served on the parent, if it is not complied with the parent will be guilty of an offence unless he can satisfy the court that he has a reasonable excuse for non-compliance. If prosecuted, the parent will face the same penalties as are outlined above.[25]

Reasonable Excuses

10–14   Throughout the discussion on whether a child has failed to attend school regularly, there is reference to "reasonable excuses" which, if established, may prevent a criminal prosecution or conviction and avoid the need for an attendance order or a referral to the reporter. What then constitutes a reasonable excuse? This is laid down in statute. The Education

---

[22] Education (Scotland) Act 1980, s. 39(3).
[23] Education (Scotland) Act 1980, s. 39(4).
[24] Education (Scotland) Act 1980, s. 40.
[25] Education (Scotland) Act 1980, s. 41.

(Scotland) Act 1980 stipulates that the following situations will be deemed to be "reasonable excuses" for failing to attend school:

(1) There is no school within walking distance of the child's home and the education authority has not provided school transport or other appropriate arrangements to enable the child to attend school regularly. If, however, as a result of his parent's placing request a child has been admitted to a school which is more than walking distance from his home, then the authority has no obligation to provide transport and, accordingly, lack of school transport in these circumstances would not be a reasonable excuse.[26]

(2) The child has been ill and therefore unable to attend school. It should be noted that in such a case, the authority may ask for the child to be examined by a doctor and the parent must allow this. If he does not, then he will be guilty of an offence and may be prosecuted as outlined above.[27]

(3) There are other circumstances which in the opinion of the education authority or the court afford a reasonable excuse.

There is little reported case law on precisely what "other **10–15** circumstances" would be accepted as constituting a reasonable excuse. In one case, a father who lived a little over a mile from the local village school was prosecuted because of the failure of his children, aged eight and five, to attend that school regularly. The road between home and school was a main road without pavements. Although the father could deliver the children to school in the morning, he could not collect them in the afternoon because of his job. His wife did not work, but had a three-and-a-half-year-old child to care for. If she were to collect the children, she would need to take this younger child with her. The sheriff recognised the father's dilemma. It would, he said, be "most imprudent" for the parents to allow their children to walk home alone, nor could the

---

[26] Education (Scotland) Act 1980, s. 42(1) and (1A). See also Chapters 5 and 7.
[27] Education (Scotland) Act 1980, s. 42(3).

mother be expected to take the younger child with her to school "in all weathers". Accordingly, he decided that the parents' "inability to make their own arrangements for their children to be brought safely back from school are circumstances which afford [the parent] a reasonable excuse for not sending his children to school."[28]

10–16   A later English case involving school transport concerned a child who lived 2.8 miles from his school and was therefore within walking distance according to the legal definition. His route to school was along an unlit country road used by milk lorries and cattle wagons. Until he was eight years old, the authority had provided transport to school but then withdrew it. The authority took the view that the child could use the route safely if accompanied and they were not satisfied that it was not reasonably practicable for one of the child's parents to accompany him. The court held that it was for an education authority, in the circumstances of each case, to decide whether free transport was necessary in order to facilitate the attendance at school of the child concerned. In this particular case, there was material on which the authority could validly conclude that it was practicable for the child to be accompanied and it was reasonable for him to be accompanied to school.[29]

10–17   Further guidance on other circumstances which would constitute a reasonable excuse for non-attendance is given by the Scottish Office Education Department.[30] Authorised absences would include, for example, medical and dental treatment, bereavement, study leave for external examinations, religious observance, family holidays where attendance is otherwise satisfactory, certified debates and other activities not arranged by the school, extended visits overseas to relatives and sanctioned extended absence in relation to children of travelling families. Although these categories are quite specific, an authority still needs to consider the circumstances of each case when deciding on reasonableness. Where appropriate, permission should be sought in advance of the proposed absence to avoid action for non-attendance being initiated.

[28] *Skeen v. Tunnah*, 1970 S.L.T. (Sh. Ct.) 66, at p. 67.
[29] *R. v. Devon County Council, ex p. G.* [1988] 3 W.L.R. 1386 (H.L.).
[30] See Circular No. 1/95, para. 6.3.

While the above indicate what will constitute a reasonable   **10–18**
excuse, the Act does specify a particular circumstance which
will not be accepted as such. If a child has been excluded
from school because of his parent's refusal to comply with
school rules then, unless a court decides otherwise, he will be
considered to have failed to attend school without reasonable
cause.[31] The parent will then be subject to prosecution notwithstanding the exclusion.

Exemption from School Attendance

It is possible for an education authority to exempt a child from   **10–19**
the obligation to attend school. This applies only to children
aged 14 years or over, where the authority is satisfied after
investigation that, because of circumstances at home, it would
cause exceptional hardship to insist that the child attends
school. The exemption is granted to allow the child to help at
home. So, for example, if a parent became ill and there was
no one else to care for him, or to look after younger children
in the family, the authority can be asked to exercise its discretion in this way. Conditions can be imposed with the exemption regarding further attendance at school until the child is
16. Such an exemption can only last until the next school starting date, which would be the beginning of the next autumn
term. If appropriate, however, an exemption can be renewed.
Where an exemption has been granted, the child's parents
cannot be prosecuted or have any other proceeding brought
against them in respect of their child's failure to attend
school.[32]

Attendance Register

It should be noted that a register of admissions and with-   **10–20**
drawals must be kept at every school in respect of each
school year. In addition, an attendance register must be kept

---

[31] Education (Scotland) Act 1980, s. 35(2). See *Wyatt v. Wilson*, 1992 S.L.T.
1135.
[32] Education (Scotland) Act 1980, s. 34.

and this will contain the name of every pupil who has been admitted but not withdrawn from the school. Headteachers must ensure that a record is kept of pupils' absences in respect of each morning and afternoon of every school day. For the purpose of the attendance register an absent pupil will be "deemed" to be present if he is absent in circumstances approved by the education authority and complies with any condition attached to that approval. This would cover, for example, work experience or educational visits where the pupil is not physically present in school, but specifically does not cover absence due to sickness or exemption granted on hardship grounds.[33]

10–21 The keeping of the attendance register is of particular significance as a certificate giving details of a child's attendance record and signed by the headteacher can be used in any legal proceedings. Unless the contrary can be proved, the certificate will be accepted as sufficient evidence of the child's attendance at school.[34]

---

[33] The Schools General (Scotland) Regulations 1975 (S.I. 1975 No. 1135) as amended, reg. 9 and Sched. 1.
[34] Education (Scotland) Act 1980, s. 86(c).

CHAPTER 11

DISCIPLINE

Schools are complex organisations and complex organisa- 11–01
tions need to regulate the behaviour of people in them. If rules
are broken by a pupil then action, of varying degrees of sever-
ity, can be taken by school staff. This chapter looks at what
action staff can properly take as, at least in some areas, there
are strict rules governing when and how sanctions can be
administered. Interestingly, the Final Report of the Working
Group on Corporal Punishment commissioned by the Convention of Scottish Local Authorities listed 21 different sanctions
employed, ranging from disapproving gestures to exclusion!
It is obviously important, therefore, for parents, pupils and
staff to know where the lines can be drawn.

Corporal Punishment

Until comparatively recently, corporal punishment, if not over- 11–02
enthusiastically administered, was an accepted, if not always
welcomed, type of chastisement in Scottish schools. However,
a change in the law was introduced by the Education (No. 2)
Act 1986, which amended the Education (Scotland) Act 1980.
What that Act said was that "Where, in any proceedings, it is
shown that corporal punishment has been given to a pupil by
or on the authority of a member of the staff, giving the punishment cannot be justified on the ground that it was done in
pursuance of a right exercisable by the member of staff by
virtue of his position as such."[1] In short, a teacher who gives
corporal punishment can be sued for damages and his status
as a teacher is no defence. The Act did not make giving corporal punishment a criminal offence, however. It stated spe-

[1] Education (Scotland) Act 1980, s. 48A(1).

63

cifically that "A person does not commit an offence by reason of any conduct relating to a pupil which would, apart from this section, be justified on the ground that it was done in pursuance of a right exercisable by a member of the staff by virtue of his position as such."[2] The Act, usefully, goes on to define what corporal punishment is as follows: "doing anything for the purposes of punishing the pupil concerned (whether or not there are also other reasons for doing it) which, apart from any justification, would constitute physical assault upon the person."[3] So, if corporal punishment were to be administered, provided that the behaviour merited it and the punishment was not excessive, no criminal offence would be committed.

11–03   Of course, not all situations are simple and there will be times when a cautionary word is not enough to deal with a situation where immediate action is called for. For example, pupils may simply not stop fighting and have to be separated. The Act attempts to cater for this type of situation. What it says is that "A person is not to be taken for the purposes of this section as giving corporal punishment by virtue of anything done for reasons which include averting an immediate danger of personal injury to, or an immediate danger to the property of, any person (including the pupil concerned)."[4] So if a teacher pulls apart two battling pupils and restrains them from renewing the affray then, provided reasonable force is used, he is not taken as giving corporal punishment and is therefore not guilty of assault.

These provisions apply not only to schools managed by education authorities but also to any other place where they provide school education.[5]

11–04   It is conceivable that, despite the possibility of being sued, a teacher may give a pupil corporal punishment. In that event, a parent would be well advised to report the matter to the education authority because it is likely that it will have forbidden the use of that punishment, as many authorities had even

---

[2] Education (Scotland) Act 1980, s. 48A(4).
[3] Education (Scotland) Act 1980, s. 48A(2).
[4] Education (Scotland) Act 1980, s. 48A(3).
[5] Education (Scotland) Act 1980, s. 48A(5).

before the 1986 Act was passed. If it had, then in the event of it being sued because a teacher has given corporal punishment, it will be very likely to succeed in defending the case. The teacher would in that case have to bear any damages awarded against him. Also, disciplinary action would be likely to follow by the authority against the teacher if there was sufficient evidence to justify it. However, a recent case in Derbyshire has introduced a new element into this subject. A teacher was dismissed for allegedly smacking two children and forcing another to sit beneath a desk. She denied smacking but admitted tapping a child to get his attention. It was the first complaint against her in 21 years of teaching. She raised a case of wrongful dismissal at an industrial tribunal and won. She was awarded £6,800 compensation although she was not reinstated. Whilst each case must be decided on its own facts, this one will be in the minds of education authorities if faced with similar allegations.[6]

Exclusion from School

The first thing to say about exclusion of a pupil from school **11–05** is that it involves a tightly-regulated procedure and must not be confused with "suspension". Suspension of a pupil used to be within the power of a headteacher but since there are now regulations governing exclusion, it is thought that sending a pupil home as a disciplinary measure can only be done under the rules relating to exclusion. It is a very serious step to take and is only likely to be done, in the main, after other approaches to the problem have been tried.

There are only two grounds upon which an authority may **11–06** exclude a pupil. They are: (a) if it is of the opinion that the parent of the pupil refuses or fails to comply, or to allow the pupil to comply, with the rules, regulations or disciplinary requirements of the school; or (b) if it considers that in all the circumstances to allow the pupil to continue his attendance at the school would be likely to be seriously detrimental to

---

[6] *The Times Educational Supplement*, Sept. 18, 1992, p. 10.

order and discipline in the school or the educational wellbeing of the pupils there.[7]

11–07   It should be noted that the first ground relates to the actions of the parent of a pupil whilst the second relates to that of the pupil himself. Not every act of indiscipline by a pupil will merit exclusion. It must be serious enough to have either of the effects referred to and, as there is an appeal available, the education authority must be able to prove its case if it is to succeed in justifying its action.

11–08   If a decision has been taken to exclude a child from school, he is not simply sent home and that is an end of it. Certain procedures must be gone through. On the same day that the decision to exclude a child has been taken, the authority must tell the parent, either orally or in writing, about the decision. It must also give a date, time and place where someone representing the authority will be available to discuss the decision. The date must be within seven days after the date when the decision was taken. If the pupil is 16 years old or over, the intimation must be made to him and any discussions following take place with him. What happens next depends upon whether or not the decision to exclude the pupil is accepted and whether or not the pupil has been re-admitted to school within seven days of the date of the decision to exclude him.

11–09   If a pupil has not been re-admitted to his school within eight days of the date of the decision to exclude him or if he (if aged 16 or over) or his parent has not told the headteacher that he neither wishes to appeal nor to take the matter further in any other way, then the authority must send to the pupil or parent respectively the following information: (a) the reasons for the decision to exclude; (b) the conditions, if any, with which the pupil and his parent or either the pupil or his parent are required to comply or to undertake to comply as conditions precedent to the pupil being re-admitted to the school; (c) the right to refer the decision under section 28H of the Education (Scotland) Act 1980 to an appeal committee set up and maintained under section 28D of that Act; (d) the address to which such a reference should be made; and (e) any other

---

[7] Schools General (Scotland) Regulations 1975, reg. 4 as amended.

information which the education authority considers appropriate.

This may be sent by post or handed to the parent, or the **11–10** pupil himself if aged 16 or over. The authority may provide this information in respect of any other pupil who has been excluded (for example, if an appeal has been lodged) and again, if it decides to do so, it may be done within eight days immediately following the date of the decision to exclude him or thereafter. There is nothing to prevent this information being included in the original letter advising that a pupil has been excluded, although an authority might wish a day or two to determine the conditions upon which re-admission could take place. There is a right to refer a decision to exclude a pupil to an appeal committee. The appeal committee may confirm or annul the decision to exclude. If conditions have been attached to a pupil's re-admission, it may confirm or modify them. The decision of an appeal must be complied with by an education authority. An appeal against a decision of an appeal committee lies to the sheriff, who may confirm or annul the decision to exclude or modify any conditions. The sheriff's decision is final.[8]

Where an exclusion has been ordered, it must be entered **11–11** on a pupil's progress record (see Chapter 9) together with details of any decision of an appeal committee or sheriff on it. The parent (or young person) must be informed of the terms of the entry as soon as practicable. If, however, the exclusion was annulled by either the appeal committee or the sheriff, the regulations themselves do not authorise the disclosure of the original decision to exclude the pupil to anyone entitled to access the progress record.[9]

The parent of a pupil who has been excluded from school **11–12** and who is not later re-admitted is not freed of his obligation to provide efficient education. He must find a means to do that other than through the school from which the child was excluded.[10]

---

[8] Schools General (Scotland) Regulations 1975, reg. 4A and Education (Scotland) Act 1980, s. 28H.

[9] Schools General (Scotland) Regulations 1975, reg. 10 as amended.

[10] See also Chapter 1 regarding the duty of parents to educate.

Detention

Detention after closure of school

11–13　The detention of pupils after school hours is not based on any authority given by Act of Parliament or regulation, unlike the exclusion of pupils. If it is to be justified at all, it must be on the grounds that it is within the power which the common law allows to teachers. If a parent consents to his child's detention for a reasonable length of time, then it would be hard to say that it was not permissible. However, if a parent either refused consent or was simply not consulted, the position may be different.

11–14　What has to be decided is when the authority of a teacher over a pupil ends. If it is when the school day has ended, then there would seem to be no justification for detaining a pupil after that point. A leading writer has said that "a school teacher may detain and restrict the free movement of a child or young person or ward so far as is reasonable and necessary in the interests of discipline and training or the ward's own safety".[11] However, it could be argued that that only applies within the normal school day although a definite statement to that effect is difficult to make. The same writer also says that "The slightest interference with the personal liberty of an individual which is not warranted by the law will justify an *actio injuriarum* for solatium", *i.e.* the person detained can sue the person who detained him. There is also support, in an English case, for the idea that detention after school is not permissible. In it, it was stated that "By the law of this country no man can be restrained of his liberty without authority in law."[12] So while the position cannot be stated with complete confidence, it is thought that the balance comes down on the side of a teacher having no authority to detain a pupil after school.

Detention during school hours

11–15　For the reasons given in the last paragraph, it is thought that a teacher cannot detain a pupil during the lunch break if that

---

[11] D. M. Walker, *The Law of Delict in Scotland* (2nd ed.), p. 685.
[12] *Herd v. Weardale Steel, Coke and Coal Co. Ltd.* [1915] A.C. 67 (H.L.).

pupil normally goes home, or somewhere else outwith school, for lunch. Would that still be the case if lunch was normally taken in school? The answer is very probably yes, as the lunch break cannot properly be said to be part of the school day. Detention during a morning or afternoon break would be quite in order though, because they are both part of the school day.

Supervision during detention
Schools must take reasonable care of the pupils in their charge. This principle applies during a period of detention in the same way as it does to any other time which a pupil spends in school. Supervision is dealt with in detail in Chapter 16. 11–16

Other Punishments

Apart from those already dealt with, there are a number of punishments which a school may impose. The old faithful one of giving lines is quite justifiable, but the material should have an educational content. Withdrawal of privilege such as not being allowed to participate in a school club for a time would also be in order. If a pupil was disrupting a lesson by, *e.g.* playing a radio, then a teacher would be quite entitled to remove it although it would have to be returned at the end of the school day. If a pupil were to be found carrying a weapon of some sort, perhaps a knife, then that should be removed and retained for the parent to collect. It might also be appropriate to refer the matter to the reporter to the children's panel. 11–17

Civil Liability of Pupils

Children being what they are, they sometimes wilfully or negligently cause damage to persons and property. That can happen in a school as well as in the home. Whether or not they can successfully be sued depends on the circumstances of the event and also on the child simply being old enough (age 14 and over for boys, age 12 and over for girls). Parents 11–18 are not themselves automatically responsible for their children's wrongdoing while in school, although if a child had been instructed by his parent to throw a stone through the headteacher's office window then the parent would probably be found liable.[13] The most important thing to think about when considering suing a child is that children generally have no money or insurance. Whilst a request to repay the cost of damage could be made, it is most unlikely that it could be enforced and other means of punishment will generally have to be sought.

Children's Panel

11–19 This chapter is about punishment. That is not what the children's panel is about. It deals with children who are in need of compulsory measures of care, and punishment and compulsory care are very different things. Mention of the children's panel is only included in this chapter because there are some things which can happen in the life of a child which might perhaps in former times have caused a child to be punished but now cause them to be the subject of compulsory measures of care. There are a number of grounds upon which a child can be referred to the reporter to the children's panel. The ones which are of particular interest for children in school, although there are others, are as follows: (a) if a child has failed to attend school regularly without reasonable excuse; (b) if a child has committed an offence; (c) if a child has misused a volatile substance by deliberately inhaling, other than for medicinal purposes, that substance's vapour.[14]

11–20 Anyone, including a teacher, can refer a child to the reporter for any of these matters. It cannot be stressed too strongly that not every child who, *e.g.* is caught sniffing glue, will be referred to the reporter. Other types of action will most likely take place first. The parent will almost certainly be informed. The social work department may be asked to take an interest. At the end of the day though, a reference to the

---

[13] D. M. Walker, *Principles of Scottish Private Law* (4th ed.), vol. 1, p. 217.
[14] Social Work (Scotland) Act 1968, s. 32 as amended.

reporter is possible and, in the case of truancy, the parent may also be prosecuted in court. If a child's behaviour appears to be of a criminal nature, then the police may well become involved.

CHAPTER 12

RELIGIOUS EDUCATION

12–01 Historically, it has been the custom for religious observance to be practised and instruction in religion to be provided in Scottish schools. Modern statute law reflects this tradition by allowing education authorities to continue this provision. Indeed, it is unlawful for an education authority to discontinue religious observance or instruction unless the proposal to do so has been the subject of a poll of the local government electors in the area concerned and has been approved by the majority of those voters.[1]

12–02 Although every school run by the education authority must be open to pupils of all denominations, the law provides a "conscience clause" whereby a parent may withdraw his child from any instruction in religious subjects and from any religious observance in the school. It is also laid down that no pupil must be placed at any disadvantage as regards his secular education at the school either because he has been withdrawn from such classes or because of the denomination to which he or his parent belongs.[2]

12–03 There is a corresponding provision intended to safeguard religious beliefs although this relates only to children who are boarders at a school or other educational establishment managed by the education authority. If the parent of such a pupil asks for his child to be allowed to attend worship of a particular denomination on Sundays or other significant occasions, then the authority must make arrangements to ensure that the child has reasonable opportunities to do so. The same applies if the parent wishes his child to receive religious instruction or otherwise to practice his religion outwith normal school hours. In making the appropriate arrangements, the authority

[1] Education (Scotland) Act 1980, s. 8(1) and (2).
[2] Education (Scotland) Act 1980, s. 9.

may provide facilities on the premises of the school for such worship or instruction. The authority must not, however, incur any expense as a result of making such arrangements.[3]

12–04 Guidance as to the provision of religious education and observance in both primary and secondary schools has been issued by the Education Department of the Scottish Office.[4] In general, religious education in all schools should be based on Christianity, this being the main religious tradition in Scotland, but the syllabus should also take account of the teaching and practices of other religions. It should aim to promote understanding and respect for others' beliefs. This would be particularly important in schools where there are significant numbers of children from non-Christian backgrounds.

12–05 Religious observance is seen to complement instruction in religion and to have an important role in schools. In non-denominational schools, such observance would be of a broadly Christian nature. A denominational school, although under the management of the education authority, would of course provide its own particular form of worship. Similarly, in schools where there are pupils from a range of ethnic backgrounds, it may be appropriate for the school to arrange particular forms of observance for the different religious groups. Many education authorities and schools will have formulated policy guidelines on the provision and content of religious education and observance and, accordingly, information could be obtained locally by parents concerned about this aspect of their child's education.[5]

Religious Education in Primary Schools

12–06 The Scottish Office recommends that a minimum of 10 per cent of curriculum time be set aside for religious and moral education. Although some aspects of moral education will occasionally fall within other areas of the curriculum, this should not detract from the time to be allowed specifically for

---

[3] Education (Scotland) Act 1980, s. 10.
[4] Scottish Office Education Department Circular No. 6/91.
[5] Circular No. 6/91, paras. 4, 6 and 7.

the subject of religious and moral education. It is recommended that all pupils should take part in religious observance not less than once a week. The nature of the observance will be determined by school policy which will itself be formulated by such factors as the religions practised by the pupils in the school and perhaps the availability of accommodation. Accordingly, forms of worship may be provided for distinct groups, for individual classes or for the whole school.[6]

Religious Education in Secondary Schools

12–07 The recommendation here is that a minimum of 5 per cent of curriculum time should be spent on religious and moral education in S1/S2, a minimum of 80 hours over two years in S3 and S4 and "a continuing element within the context of personal and social development" for all pupils in S5 and S6. In addition, it is considered desirable that pupils be given the opportunity to follow courses in religious studies which lead to a qualification such as the Scottish Certificate of Education. At secondary level, it is hoped that all pupils will take part in religious observance at least once a month. Again, the form of such observance will be determined by school policy.[7]

12–08 In order to fulfil the requirement to teach religious studies as part of the curriculum, authorities must have regard to the need for specialist teachers. It is also possible for existing teachers of other subjects to undertake courses whereby they are trained to teach religious education. This may be of particular importance in non-denominational schools.[8]

12–09 Denominational schools, although under the management of the education authority, are conducted in the interest of a particular church or religious body, reflecting the religious beliefs of the parents whose children attend them. As a result, applicants for any teaching post in such a school must be approved by representatives of the appropriate church as regards their religious belief and character.[9]

---

[6] Circular No. 6/91, paras. 8 and 9.
[7] Circular No. 6/91, paras. 10 and 11.
[8] Circular No. 6/91, para. 13.
[9] Education (Scotland) Act 1980, s. 21(2A).

The Role of Chaplains in Schools

For every denominational school, the authority must appoint **12–10** an unpaid supervisor of religious instruction, approved by the relevant church. This would normally be the local priest or other appropriate minister, who would oversee the religious instruction and observance.[10] It is the norm also for non-denominational schools to have a designated chaplain, again usually one of the local ministers. His involvement would largely be in the planning and conduct of worship, in carrying out pastoral duties with staff and pupils and perhaps assisting in the particular school's educational programme.[11]

---

[10] Education (Scotland) Act 1980, s. 21(3).
[11] Scottish Office Education Department Circular No. 6/91, para. 12. Generally, see Chapter 5 on denominational schools.

CHAPTER 13

CHILDREN WITH SPECIAL EDUCATIONAL NEEDS

Introduction

13–01 The law which applies to the education of children with special educational needs is quite involved. It is difficult to think of another branch of the law relating to education which matches its close regulation. The rights of parents are heavily emphasised. The duties placed on education authorities are set out in detail. Chronologically, the first thing which education authorities must do is to disseminate information regarding the importance of the early discovery of special educational needs and the opportunity for assessment available.[1]

What are "Special Educational Needs"?

13–02 Special educational needs are needs caused by a learning difficulty which a child or young person has which call for provision for special educational needs to be made for him. A child or young person has a learning difficulty if: (i) he has significantly greater difficulty in learning than the majority of children or young persons of his age; or (ii) he suffers from a disability which either prevents or hinders him from making use of educational facilities of a kind generally provided for children or young persons of his age in schools under the management of the education authority of the area to which he belongs; or (iii) he is under the age of five years and is, or would be if provision for special educational needs were not made for him, likely to fall within (i) or (ii) above when over that age. For some children, the language of the home will not be the same as the language of the school. That, in itself,

---

[1] Education (Scotland) Act 1980, s. 60(1).

does not mean that a child will be taken to have special educational needs.[2]

Duties of Education Authority

Education authorities have a duty to secure that there is made for their areas adequate and efficient provision of school education. That includes making provision for children with special educational needs. What that means is that the authority must make, where necessary, educational provision which is additional to, or otherwise different from, the educational provision made generally for children or young persons of that age.[3] The duty is owed to children who are of school age or young persons belonging to the area of the education authority. Authorities must establish which children have pronounced, specific or complex special educational needs which need continuing review and keep a record of needs in respect of each.[4]   **13–03**

Authorities are also under a duty in respect of children in their area who are at least two years old. If any such children come to the attention of the authority as having, or appearing to have, special educational needs, then the authority must keep a record of needs for them if the needs are such as to require continuing review. Authorities also have a general power to establish whether any children under the age of two have such special educational needs as require a record of needs to be kept. The same power exists in respect of young persons but can only be exercised if the parent or the young person himself asks for it to be used.[5] Even then, as it is a power to act and not a duty, an authority need not take any action.   **13–04**

The next area which needs to be looked at is how the process of determining whether or not a child has special educational needs actually works.   **13–05**

---

[2] Education (Scotland) Act 1980, s. 1(5)(*d*).
[3] Education (Scotland) Act 1980, s. 61(5)(*c*).
[4] Education (Scotland) Act 1980, s. 60(2)(*b*).
[5] Education (Scotland) Act 1980, s. 60(2)(*a*) and (*b*) and (5).

Observation and Assessment

13–06   Before a child can be recorded, *i.e.* have a record of needs opened and kept for him, his parent must be invited by notice in writing to submit him for assessment. The notice must give the following information:

(a)   That the purpose of any examinations held in connection with the assessment is to afford to the education authority advice as to his special educational needs and whether or not they ought to record the child.

(b)   The times and places at which any examination will be held.

(c)   That the parent has the right to be present at any medical examinations.

(d)   The name of the officer of the authority from whom advice and further information may be obtained.

(e)   That the parent has the opportunity to express to the authority, within 21 days from the date of the notice or such longer period as the notice may specify, his views as regards the special educational needs of the child, and the measures required to meet those needs.[6]

13–07   If the parent does not submit the child for assessment, the authority serves a further notice requiring the child to be submitted. It may only do that, however, if the child is one in respect of whom the authority has a duty to establish whether a record of needs should be opened. The same information as in the first notice must be given. In addition, the parent must be advised that failure to comply with the notice without reasonable excuse will cause him to be guilty of an offence and liable to a fine.[7] If the child is still not submitted for assessment, then the authority is no longer under any duty to establish whether or not he has needs which would require a record of needs to be opened.[8]

13–08   Parents have the right to ask that their child undergoes the process of observation and assessment. However, an authority may refuse to have that done if it considers that in its opin-

[6] Education (Scotland) Act 1980, s. 61(5).

[7] Education (Scotland) Act 1980, s. 61(3) and (4).

[8] Education (Scotland) Act 1980, s. 61(5).

ion the request is unreasonable. There is no express right of appeal given to parents against such a decision.

Young Persons

Before a young person can be recorded he must have under- **13–09** gone the process of observation and assessment. He must also have been given the opportunity by the authority to express his views by notice in writing. The notice must give at least 14 days from its date for the young person to give his views on his special educational needs and what is required to meet them. If the authority is satisfied that the young person is incapable of expressing his views, then his parent must be given the same notice and chance to comment.[9]

The Decision to Record

In deciding whether or not to record a child or young person, **13–10** the authority must take into consideration the following:
(a)   The advice given to them following the process of observation and assessment.
(b)   Any views expressed by the child's parent, the young person, or his parent where he is incapable of expressing them himself.
(c)   Any reports or other information from any school which he has attended which was not under its management.
(d)   Any other reports or information relevant to his educational needs which it is able to obtain.

Once the decision to record a child or young person has **13–11** been taken, notice must be served on the child's parent, young person, or young person's parent (as appropriate) to that effect, specifying the terms in which the recording is proposed. The notice should state that views may be expressed on the terms of the recording within 14 days of the date of the notice. Thereafter, the authority must give further notice of its decision as to those terms, the right of appeal and the

[9] Education (Scotland) Act 1980, s. 61(7).

name and address of the person to whom application may be made for advice and information about the child's or young person's special educational needs (unless the authority has been asked not to appoint one). Equally, a decision not to record must be intimated by notice in writing and must give details of the right of appeal.[10]

13–12   After a child or young person has been recorded, provision for his special educational needs must be made by the authority. In the case of children who are two years of age or over, but do not yet attend school, the authority must make suitable arrangements for any special educational needs which have been recorded and which are not otherwise being met.[11]

13–13   A child's needs may be capable of being met in different ways. For example, it may be that an authority can quite adequately meet them in the local school with, perhaps, extra support being provided there. It may be that a parent would prefer his child to attend a private school which could equally well meet the child's needs. In that event, the authority will have discharged its duty by offering to place the child in the local school. That is not to say that children can always be catered for in that way. Some have needs which authorities simply cannot meet in mainstream or special schools and, in such cases, private provision will be made at the expense of the authority.

Reviewing Decisions to Record

13–14   Once a child or young person has been recorded, the education authority must, from time to time, review both the decision to record and the information contained in the record of needs. It must also do this if requested to do so by the parent or young person (or his parent, where the authority is of the opinion that he is incapable of expressing his views) in writing. Before a request for a review can be granted, 12 months must

---

[10] Education (Scotland) Act 1980, s. 62(1) and (2).
[11] Education (Scotland) Act 1980, s. 62(3).

have elapsed since the date either of the decision to record, or of the last review.[12]

Appeal Procedure

An appeal can be made by the parent of a recorded child in **13–15** respect of a number of decisions of an authority. The appeal takes the form of a referral to an appeal committee. The decisions which can be referred are as follows:

(a) A decision of an education authority to record a child or, following a review of the decision to record him, to continue to record him, or a decision of the authority not to record the child or, following a review of the decision to record, not to continue to record him.

(b) The authority's decision as to the terms in which the summary of a child's impairments or the statement of his special educational needs is recorded in his record of needs or any such decisions following a review.

(c) The authority's decision as to the nomination of a school to be attended by the recorded child, or the recorded young person, or any such decision following a review of the decision to record provided a placing request has been made by the parent or the young person.

(d) The authority's decision refusing a placing request in respect of the child.

There are rights of appeal in respect of young persons too. **13–16** If the young person is capable of expressing his views, then he may exercise those rights. If he cannot, then his parent may do so on his behalf. The right of appeal covers those matters dealt with in (b) to (d). An appeal may also be made against a decision of an authority not to record or, following a review, not to continue to record a young person.

There is a time restriction on referrals made concerning (c) **13–17** and (d) above. Once a referral to an appeal committee has been made, no further one can be made on the same grounds

[12] Education (Scotland) Act 1980, s. 65A.

for one year beginning with the date on which the previous reference was made.

13–18 Any reference must be made to the appeal committee within 28 days of having received the decision of the education authority regarding the terms in which the recording is to be made. The committee can allow a reference to be lodged late if it thinks that good cause has been shown to allow it. Anyone lodging a late reference should take care to set out what he thinks is a good reason why it should still be considered.[13]

13–19 Appeal committees cannot deal with everything which is referred to them on their own. Some matters must be referred to the Secretary of State for him to decide. They are:

(1) A reference concerning the authority's decision to record or not to record a child or to continue to record him.

(2) A reference concerning the authority's decision as to the terms in which the summary of a child's or young person's impairments or the statement of his special educational needs are recorded.

(3) A reference concerning a decision of an education authority not to record a young person or not to continue to record him.

(4) Where the appeal committee considers that it cannot deal with a reference of the authority's decision as to the nomination of a school to be attended by the child or young person without having the decision of the Secretary of State on the question of whether or not the child should be recorded or, in the case of either a child or young person, on the terms in which the summary of impairments or the statement of special educational needs are recorded.

13–20 The Secretary of State has several options open to him. He may either confirm the authority's decision or refuse to do so, or he may confirm it with modifications. Authorities must comply with his decision. He must obtain and consider the views of the parent who made the reference to the appeal committee before refusing to confirm an authority's decision to record, or continue to record, a child. He must also obtain and consider the views of the parent or young person before

---

[13] Education (Scotland) Act 1980, s. 63(1)–(5); see also Appendix 5 *re* appeal committees.

confirming, with modifications, an authority's decision as to the terms in which the child's or young person's impairments, or the statement of the special educational needs arising from those impairments, are recorded.

Once the Secretary of State has made his decision, he must **13–21** notify the appeal committee, the education authority and the person who made the reference to the appeal committee. An appeal committee must then reach its decision as to the school which the child will attend in the light of the decision of the Secretary of State.[14]

Placing Requests for Children with Special Educational Needs

A parent of a recorded child can make a placing request to **13–22** have his child educated in a school under the management of an education authority (not necessarily the authority in whose area they live) or in a special school which is willing to admit the child. If the school is one which it manages, the authority is under a duty to admit the child. In the case of a special school being specified, the authority (and in this case the authority must be the "home" authority of the parent) must meet the fees and other necessary costs of the child's attendance at the school.

There are circumstances where this duty does not apply, **13–23** however. In the first place, if more than one school is named, then the request is deemed to apply to the school which is named first. The other grounds are:

(a) If placing the child in the specified school would (i) make it necessary for the authority to take an additional teacher into employment; (ii) give rise to significant expenditure on extending or otherwise altering the accommodation at or facilities provided in connection with the school; (iii) be seriously detrimental to the continuity of the child's education; or (iv) be likely to be seriously detrimental to order and discipline in the school or the educational wellbeing of the pupils there.

---

[14] Education (Scotland) Act 1980, s. 64(1)–(9).

(b) If the education normally provided at the specified school is not suited to the age, ability or aptitude of the child.

(c) If the education authority has already required the child to discontinue his attendance at the specified school.

(d) If, where the specified school is a special school, the child does not have special educational needs requiring the education or special facilities normally provided at the school.

(e) If the specified school is a single sex school (within the meaning given to that expression by section 26 of the Sex Discrimination Act 1975) and the child is not of the sex admitted or taken (under that section) to be admitted to the school.

(f) If (i) the specified school is not a public school; (ii) the authority is able to make at less cost adequate provision for the special educational needs of the child in a school under its management; and (iii) the authority has offered to place the child in the school referred to in sub-paragraph (ii) above.

13–24   However, and notwithstanding any of the reasons in (a) to (f), an authority may still, if it so decides, place the child in the school to which his parent wishes him to go. An education authority must give its decision on a placing request in writing. If it decides to refuse the request, then it must give written reasons and must also inform the parent of his right to appeal to an appeal committee.[15] The parent of a recorded young person, or the young person himself, if capable of expressing his views, can make a placing request in the same way as the parent of a recorded child.[16]

Appeal to the Sheriff

13–25   There are certain circumstances in which an appeal can be made to the sheriff against a decision of an appeal committee. Education authorities cannot appeal, however, if a decision

[15] Education (Scotland) Act 1980, Sched. A2, para. 3.
[16] *ibid.*

goes against them. An appeal can be made against the decision of an education authority as to the nomination of a school to be attended by the child or young person (this will be in the record of needs) or in respect of the refusal of a placing request.[17] The procedure to be followed is that of summary application and the services of a solicitor would usually be needed.

It may be that the sheriff is asked by either the appellant or **13–26** the education authority to refer certain matters to the Secretary of State for his decision before he can come to a conclusion himself. He can only do this if the appeal committee has not done so already. The matters which he can refer are whether or not the child should be recorded, or the terms of the recording of the summary of impairments or the statement of special educational needs. Such a reference would be dealt with in the same manner as a reference from an appeal committee.[18] The sheriff must take into account the decision of the Secretary of State. Where there has been no reference to the Secretary of State, the sheriff may confirm the decision of the education authority if he is satisfied that one or more of the grounds of refusal exist and that, in all the circumstances, it is appropriate to do so. Otherwise, he shall refuse to confirm the decision of the education authority and shall require it to place the child or young person in the school which he wishes to attend and to amend the record accordingly. In that event, if the school which the child or young person wishes to attend is an independent or grant-aided school, then the sheriff must require the education authority to meet the fees and other necessary costs of attendance.[19]

Provision for Recorded Children after Leaving School

Recorded children, just like non-recorded children, do not **13–27** have to stay at school after they have reached school-leaving age. To help parents decide what is best for their child with

---

[17] Education (Scotland) Act 1980, s. 65(1).
[18] Educatioh (Scotland) Act 1980, s. 65(3) and (4).
[19] Education (Scotland) Act 1980, s. 65(6) and (7).

regard to his future, education authorities must consider what provision would benefit each recorded child in its area after he ceases to be of school age and submit a report on the outcome to the parents. This process must begin two years before the child ceases to be of school age and end nine months before that date.[20]

13–28   For the purposes of the report, it is important for the education authority to find out if the person is disabled or not. The term "disabled" is defined in law to mean "a chronically sick or disabled person, or a person suffering from mental disorder (being a person in need) to whom section 12 of the Social Work (Scotland) Act 1968 applies". Basically, the type of person covered by that section of the 1968 Act is someone who, if given assistance, would not require the social work authority to spend even more money by having to provide him with, e.g. residential care. The social work department of the authority must be consulted for its opinion on that and, if it does think that the person is disabled, that must be noted in the report. The availability of any statutory services for the person after leaving school must also be noted. If the person is over 16, he may request that the assessment is not carried out. If, because of mental or physical incapacity, the person cannot decide for himself, his parent may request that it is not carried out.[21]

13–29   Records of needs are continued for as long as a child or young person receives school education. A young person, or his parent if he is not capable of requesting it, may require the record to be discontinued.[22]

Provision Abroad

13–30   Education authorities have the power to make provision for children outwith the United Kingdom in an establishment which caters for them if they have pronounced, specific or

---

[20] Education (Scotland) Act 1980, s. 65B(1) and (2).
[21] Disabled Persons (Services, Consultation and Representation) Act 1986, ss. 13 and 16.
[22] Education (Scotland) Act 1980, s. 65C.

complex special educational needs. They do not have to be recorded. The authorities may pay the fees and also travelling, maintenance and other expenses of the child or young person. The attendance expenses of the parents or of some other person may also be paid if it would be of advantage to the child.[23]

---

[23] Education (Scotland) Act 1980, s. 65G(1)–(3) (added by the Self-Governing Schools etc. (Scotland) Act 1989, s. 71(2)).

CHAPTER 14

PROVISION FOR ADVANCED PUPILS

14–01 As has been discussed in Chapter 13 above, the Education
(Scotland) Act 1980 imposes particular duties on an education authority to identify and meet the educational needs of
children with particular disabilities or learning difficulties.
There is no such provision for children who are of above aver-
age ability for their years. It is not unusual for a child, even
before school age, to be seen as particularly bright or to have
a special talent, perhaps in music or art. When he goes to
school this may blossom even further, to the extent that the
education being provided for him seems inadequate for his
abilities. This may obviously be a source of concern for his
parents who wish to encourage their gifted child.

14–02 The first thing to remember is that it is a parent's duty to
provide efficient education for his child, whether by sending
him to school regularly or in some other way.[1] So if a child
appears to be brighter than his classmates, it may be that
the parents will decide to buy additional books or equipment,
depending on the child's particular talent, in order to work with
him and provide the stimulus and encouragement he needs
to develop his full potential. Alternatively, parents may wish to
arrange private tuition for the child in addition to the normal
school education. This would be at the parents' own expense.

14–03 It is, however, equally true that an education authority must
provide adequate education appropriate to the needs of
pupils attending its schools, having regard to their age, ability
and aptitude.[2] Accordingly, it appears that if a child shows
exceptional ability, then the authority must provide him with
the education appropriate to his needs.

14–04 In the first instance, this may simply be a question of

---

[1] Education (Scotland) Act 1980, s. 30.
[2] Education (Scotland) Act 1980, s. 1(1) and (5).

providing additional or more advanced work for the child both in class and as homework, perhaps arranging personal tuition within school hours if this is possible, or giving consideration to moving him to a higher class. Where the child's exceptional ability is in the creative arts, then it may be that he will be helped by attending extra-curricular groups within the school, or at least within the area, catering perhaps for art, music or drama. This may involve the parents in additional expense. It is of course always open to a parent to discuss his child's progress with the headteacher concerned, with a view to working out the best strategy for his future education.

There are further measures that an education authority **14–05** can take, although these are not specifically enacted to cater for gifted children. For example, an authority is empowered to "buy in" expertise if this will promote education generally, improve the educational facilities available or indeed simply improve the education provided in its area. Specifically, payments may be made by the authority to, amongst others, another education authority, the managers of any non-local-authority school, or to any person providing education or educational services.[3] Thus there is the possibility that a child could have a special tutor, or attend a particular school even outwith the local area, both at the authority's expense.

There is a further legal provision regarding the education of **14–06** pupils in exceptional circumstances. This states that where an education authority is of the opinion that, because of exceptional circumstances, a pupil cannot fully benefit from school education unless special arrangements are made for him, or that the education most suited to his needs can best be provided at a particular school, then the authority must take the necessary action to allow that child to attend an appropriate school.[4] Any arrangements under this provision may be permanent or temporary and would be made only after consultation with the parent. Travelling expenses may be paid to enable attendance at a particular school, or the child could

[3] Education (Scotland) Act 1980, s. 24(1)(a), (c) and (e).
[4] Education (Scotland) Act 1980, s. 50(1).

be accommodated at a boarding school or other institution.[5] It can be seen, therefore, that an authority has the power to finance a child's education at a school providing specialist tuition in, say, music or drama, or even at a private school for gifted children. It should be noted, however, that where a child attends a school following a placing request by the parent (see paragraph 05–07 above), the authority is not under a duty to provide specialist education in another establishment, although it may do so.[6]

14–07   It is interesting to consider the terms of this provision. Although there is a duty to meet a pupil's particular educational needs, the duty only arises where the education authority forms an opinion that exceptional circumstances exist in relation to that child. It can be argued that the formation of an opinion is a subjective matter and the Act gives no guidance as to how such an opinion is to be formed. Presumably a child would be assessed by teachers and other specialists, but the procedure could vary from authority to authority. If a parent wishes action to be taken under this section but fails to secure the agreement of the authority, there is no right of appeal although a complaint could be made to the Secretary of State, who could make an order compelling the authority to take action.[7]

14–08   The lack of positive provision for gifted children is echoed in regulations governing information which education authorities must make available to parents. This includes "arrangements (if any) made by the authority for the education of children with special aptitudes, such as for example, in music or dance."[8] There is clearly no duty imposed on education authorities to formulate policy or guidelines in this area, although some may choose to do so and must then make this information available.

14–09   Statute does provide that education authorities must, when exercising their powers and duties, have regard to the general

---

[5] Education (Scotland) Act 1980, s. 50(2).
[6] *ibid.* See also Chapter 5, para. 05–07 on placing requests.
[7] Education (Scotland) Act 1980, s. 70. See also Chapter 18 on Complaints.
[8] The Education (School and Placing Information) (Scotland) Regulations 1982 (S.I. 1982 No. 950), Sched. 1, Pt. III, para. 3(*o*).

principle that pupils are to be educated in accordance with the wishes of their parents, but only so far as is compatible with the provision of suitable education and the avoidance of unreasonable public expenditure.[9] This in itself, however, will not necessarily assist a parent who is seeking some form of specialist education for his child.

---

[9] Education (Scotland) Act 1980, s. 28.

CHAPTER 15

EMPLOYMENT OF PUPILS/PERFORMANCES BY PUPILS

15–01   Although it is accepted practice that school age children have part-time jobs, whether doing a daily paper round, or working at weekends in a local store or supermarket, it is perhaps less well known that there are legal restrictions on the employment of children. These restrictions, which concern the minimum age at which a child may be employed, the type of work he may do and the hours he may work, are imposed both by statute and by local authority byelaws.

15–02   The following provisions are laid down in statute: a child may not be employed if he is under the age of 13[1]; a child must not work before 7 a.m. or after 7 p.m. on any day[2]; a child must not work for more than two hours on any school day or any Sunday[3] and must not work during the school day[4]; a child must not be employed on work which requires him to lift, carry or move anything so heavy as to be likely to injure himself.[5] These restrictions are absolute and apply to children anywhere in Scotland.

15–03   The employment of school age children may be further curtailed by implementation of the E.U. Directive on the Protection of Young People at work. This Directive becomes effective on June 22, 1996. In addition, an education authority has the power to make byelaws affecting the employment of children in its area.[6] These will inevitably vary from place to place but

---

[1] Children and Young Persons (Scotland) Act 1937, s. 28(1)(a) substituted by the Children Act 1972, s. 1(2).
[2] Children and Young Persons (Scotland) Act 1937, s. 28(1)(c) substituted by the Children and Young Persons Act 1963, s. 34.
[3] Children and Young Persons (Scotland) Act 1937, s. 28(1)(d) and (e).
[4] Children and Young Persons (Scotland) Act 1937, s. 28(1)(b). See also Chapter 4, para. 04–11 on work experience.
[5] Children and Young Persons (Scotland) Act 1937, s. 28(1)(f).
[6] Children and Young Persons (Scotland) Act 1937, s. 28(2).

a copy of the relevant byelaws can be obtained from the authority concerned.

Education authority byelaws may be passed which (a) com- **15–04** pletely prohibit the employment of children in any specified occupation[7]; (b) allow children to be employed by their parents or guardians in light agricultural or horticultural work[8]; (c) allow children to be employed for one hour before school[9]; (d) affect the ages at which children may work, their hours of employment, prescribe rest and meals intervals, holidays and other conditions;[10] and (e) authorise children of 14 years of age and over to be employed by their parents in street trading.[11]

In addition, byelaws may specify that before a child may **15–05** be employed in a certain, or indeed in any, type of occupation, either the child, the employer, or both, must apply to the local authority for a licence. All this is to ensure that children are regulated and restricted in what, for some, may be unsuitable occupations. Byelaws may not be used to allow children to be employed in jobs which they are prevented from doing by statute but, as can be seen, they may impose further restrictions in employment which is generally open to them.[12]

If a child or young person is employed contrary to the legal **15–06** provisions then an offence is committed. The offender would not be the person employed, but might be the employer or other person who contributed to the contravention of the law. This could conceivably be a parent who failed to ensure his or her child's compliance with the law. If only the employer is charged with the offence, he has the right to involve any such other person in the proceedings and this person may be convicted of the offence. It would be a defence for the employer if he could prove that he had done all in his power to comply with the relevant provisions.[13]

---

[7] Children and Young Persons (Scotland) Act 1937, s. 28(2)(*b*).
[8] Children and Young Persons (Scotland) Act 1937, s. 28(2)(*a*)(i) substituted by the Children Act 1972, s. 1(2).
[9] Children and Young Persons (Scotland) Act 1937, s. 28(*a*)(ii) and (*b*).
[10] Children and Young Persons (Scotland) Act 1937, s. 28(2)(*c*).
[11] Children and Young Persons (Scotland) Act 1937, s. 30 as amended by the Employment Act 1989, s. 10 and Sched. 3, Pt. III, para. 9.
[12] Children and Young Persons (Scotland) Act 1937, s. 28(2).
[13] Children and Young Persons (Scotland) Act 1937, s. 31(1).

15–07   It should be noted that if a child works without payment in any undertaking which is carried on for profit, then he is still deemed to be "employed" in that business.[14] This may cover the situation where a child helps out in a family business but is not paid for it.

Employment in Entertainment

15–08 A more specific area in which there are restrictions on the employment of young people is that of entertainment. The relevant provisions, which are all statutory, are quite complex but in essence, no person under the age of 16 may take part in any public performance unless a licence is granted by the local authority in whose area the child resides. This applies to any performance for which a charge is made, which is held in licensed premises, which is broadcast, or which is recorded with a view to its being used in a broadcast or a film for public exhibition. Even if the child does not take part in the final production, he will require a licence if he takes the place of a performer in any rehearsal or other preparation for the recording of the performance.[15]

15–09   The necessary licence should be applied for by the party responsible for the production and the application must also be signed by the parent of the child involved. Each has to complete different sections of the application form.[16]

15–10   There are certain exemptions. A licence is not required (i) if in the six months prior to the relevant performance, the child has not taken part in other performances, which would otherwise have required a licence, on more than three days; or (ii) if it is a school performance, or a performance being presented by a body approved by the education authority, for which the child is not being paid (although expenses may be reimbursed). Thus the education authority may permit a local

---

[14] Children and Young Persons (Scotland) Act 1937, s. 37(*e*).
[15] Children and Young Persons Act 1963, s. 37(1) and (2) amended by the Cable and Broadcasting Act 1984, s. 57(1) and Sched. 5, para. 12.
[16] Children (Performances) Regulations 1968 (S.I. 1968 No. 1728), reg. 1(1) and (2).

amateur dramatic or operatic group to use children in its performances without the need for individual licence applications.[17]

Before granting a licence, the education authority must be   **15–11** satisfied that the child is fit to take part in the performance, that adequate arrangements have been made for his welfare during the time involved and that his education will not suffer as a result. Where necessary, a licence may be granted but subject to conditions which must be complied with. One such condition may require that any money earned by the child should be paid into the sheriff court in the name of the child, or be dealt with in a way which is approved by the local authority. Similarly, a licence will specify the times, if any, when the child may be absent from school for the purpose of the performance. This is important as the child will then be deemed to be absent with reasonable excuse in terms of the Education (Scotland) Act 1980.[18]

It must be noted that other regulations impose additional   **15–12** conditions to be met. These include the maximum hours allowed at places of performance or rehearsal; intervals for rest and meals; if appropriate, the approval of lodgings by the education authority and arrangements for the child's education. If the child is not to be accompanied by his parent or teacher, the regulations require the appointment of a person who will be in charge of the child for the period covered by the licence.[19]

Where a licence is applied for in respect of a child under   **15–13** the age of 14, this will not be granted unless:
(1) The licence is for acting and the application is accompanied by a declaration that the part the child is to play can only be played by a child of about his age.
(2) The licence is for dancing in a ballet and the application is accompanied by a declaration that the part he is to dance can only be taken by a child of about his age. In this case, the ballet concerned must not be part of an entertainment which contains anything other than ballet or opera.

[17] Children and Young Persons Act 1963, s. 37(3).
[18] Children and Young Persons Act 1963, s. 37(4)–(7).
[19] Children (Performances) Regulations 1968 (S.I. 1968 No. 1728).

(3)   The nature of the child's part in the performance is wholly or mainly musical and either the nature of the performance is also wholly or mainly musical or the performance consists only of opera or ballet.[20]

15–14   Once a licence has been granted, the person who holds it may apply to have it varied and this may be done either by the authority which granted it, or by the authority in whose area a performance is taking place. Similarly, either interested authority may vary or revoke a licence if any condition originally imposed has not been complied with or it is no longer satisfied that the child is fit for the performance or with the arrangements made for his general welfare or education. The holder of the licence must, where practicable, be given notice of the intention to vary or revoke the licence.

15–15   If an authority refuses to grant a licence, or subsequently revokes it, or if it varies a licence other than on an application by the holder, it must give its reasons in writing. An appeal can be made to the sheriff against the refusal, revocation or variation and against any condition imposed, as long as this is not a condition which the authority is required to impose.[21]

15–16   A licence may be granted to a child aged 12 or over to be trained to take part in performances of a dangerous nature, but no child may take part in a performance where his life or limbs would be endangered.[22] As with other situations, the licence can be revoked or varied if conditions are not complied with or the child is no longer fit or willing to be trained, and an appeal lies to the sheriff against any refusal, revocation or variation.[23] It is an offence to cause or procure a child or, in the case of his parent or guardian, to allow a child, to be trained or to take part in a performance in contravention of these provisions.[24]

15–17   There are general provisions which allow an authority to

---

[20] Children and Young Persons Act 1963, s. 38(1).
[21] Children and Young Persons Act 1963, s. 39.
[22] Children and Young Persons (Scotland) Act 1937, ss. 33 and 34(2) as amended by the Employment Act 1989, s. 10 and Sched. 3, Pt. III, paras. 11 and 12.
[23] Children and Young Persons Act 1963, s. 41(3).
[24] Children and Young Persons (Scotland) Act 1937, s. 34(1) as amended by the Employment Act 1989, Sched. 3, Pt. III, para. 12(a).

check whether the law regarding the employment of children is being observed, for example authority may be obtained from a magistrate for an officer of the education authority or a police constable to enter premises to make inquiries as to child employment. Again, an authorised officer or a constable may enter any broadcasting, cable programme or film studio, or a studio used for the recording of a performance with a view to its use in a broadcast, cable programme, or a film intended for public exhibition and make inquiries as to any child taking part in performances. Such a person may also enter any premises where a child is licenced to perform or to be trained for performances of a dangerous nature.[25]

An offence is committed if any person causes or, in the case of **15–18** a parent or guardian, allows a child to take part in a performance without obtaining the necessary licence, or if he fails to observe any condition imposed in the licence or deliberately makes a false statement when applying for the licence. On conviction, a fine or a term of imprisonment, or both, may be imposed.[26]

---

[25] Children and Young Persons (Scotland) Act 1937, s. 36(2)(a) and (b) substituted by the Children and Young Persons Act 1963, s. 43 and amended by the Cable and Broadcasting Act 1984, s. 57(1) and Sched. 5, para. 5(1).
[26] Children and Young Persons Act 1963, s. 40(1).

CHAPTER 16

RESPONSIBILITIES OF EDUCATION AUTHORITIES

Getting to School

16–01   Councils may arrange for school crossing patrols to be provided to help children to cross roads on their way to or from school or from one part of a school to another. They can only have patrols in place between the hours of eight in the morning and half past five in the afternoon. Councils must be satisfied that people appointed to patrol have adequate qualifications and must provide any necessary training.[1] The positioning of crossing patrols can be a source of controversy and sometimes a formula may be used to determine where the most dangerous crossings are and, therefore, where patrols should be provided. These formulae can be very complicated indeed, taking into account such things as the numbers of vehicles passing, the lighting, visibility, etc. However, as they are provided as a matter of discretion, too much reliance should not be placed on the simple operation of a formula. Other factors such a weight of parental/political feeling will also have influence.

16–02   Responsibility for an accident at a crossing where there is a patrol will depend on the facts and circumstances. Children do not always obey instructions and if they dash into a busy road in disobedience of a patroller, then an education authority would not be liable for any injuries resulting. If, however, a patroller negligently causes a child to cross in front of a vehicle to his injury, then the education authority may very well be liable for damages.

16–03   The areas near the entrances to schools can be dangerous places with cars arriving and departing and children coming and going, often in large numbers. To reduce possible acci-

---

[1] Road Traffic Regulation Act 1984, s. 26(1).

dents, education authorities may erect safety barriers at or near school entrances and may undertake work to improve the safety of any private road which is used by pupils with the consent of the owner and occupier.[2]

At School

Education authorities must take reasonable care for the safety **16–04** of pupils when under their charge. It is easy to see that pupils are in the charge of the school during break, or playtime, but there are also the periods between the children's arrival at school and the start of the school day, and from dismissal in the afternoon until, *e.g.* the school bus leaves, to be considered. There are regulations covering what is required by way of supervision in respect of certain schools. They are special schools and primary schools attended by 50 or more pupils, the number being calculated as at the previous August 31. At such schools, pupils must be supervised by at least one person who is at least 18 years of age when in a playground during any breaktime.[3] It is curious that the regulations apply to all but the smallest primary schools. It may be that it is an acknowledgment that the smaller schools will generally be situated in sparsely-populated areas where recruitment of suitable staff may be difficult, if not impossible, but it could well be argued that the duty to take reasonable care means that supervision of pupils must also take place in those smaller schools.

The position is not so clear in secondary schools. There are **16–05** no regulations requiring a playground supervisor. The general duty of care still applies. However, considering that secondary pupils are more mature and, it is to be expected, more responsible, the duty of care may be able to be discharged by, *e.g.* a teacher walking round the playground once, as opposed to having a constant presence. Taking care, it may be argued, means doing something. It is not thought that the

---

[2] Education (Scotland) Act 1980, s. 18(1)–(3).
[3] The Schools (Safety and Supervision of Pupils) (Scotland) Regulations 1990 (S.I. 1990 No. 295).

duty can be discharged by not exercising any supervision at all, even in secondary schools. Pupils arrive at school, generally, before the bell goes. For those who make their own way to school, it could be argued that it is the responsibility of their parents to secure that they are supervised until they actually enter the school building. However, many pupils arrive at school before school begins on transport provided by the education authority. In the case of primary school children, it could well be argued that the duty of care requires supervision from the moment the transport arrives until the school begins and conversely at the end of the day. With regard to secondary school pupils, the position is not so clear, but it could again be argued that the presence of an adult is required during those times.

16–06   Primary school children certainly require constant supervision during mealtimes. Secondary pupils also require supervision, although constant supervision may not be necessary, given their age and relative maturity.

Provision of Buildings and Equipment

16–07   Education authorities have a duty to provide and maintain sufficient accommodation in schools to enable them to carry out their functions and enlarge such accommodation where necessary. They may also alter, improve, and equip their schools. They may even provide and maintain houses and hostels for teachers and other officers in their employment and may furnish them.[4]

16–08   Education authorities may also provide new denominational schools if satisfied that one is required, having regard to the religious beliefs of parents resident in the area.[5]

General Welfare of Pupils

Health

16–09   It is part of the human condition that people become ill and diseases can spread quickly amongst children in a school.

---

[4] Education (Scotland) Act 1980, s. 17(1) and (3)–(5).
[5] Education (Scotland) Act 1980, s. 17(2).

Closing a school to prevent the spread of disease or some other danger to health is most unusual, but that has to be done if a designated medical officer so advises. On a lesser scale, pupils may be excluded from school (and if the school is a boarding school, kept in the boarding facility!) on the advice of such a person for the same reasons.[6]

Cleanliness of pupils
Ensuring that pupils who attend school do so in a clean **16–10** condition is also a matter of concern to education authorities. They have the power to direct that all pupils or any individual pupil attending one or all of their schools, be inspected by a medical officer of the health board. They may do so if the medical officer considers that this is necessary in the interests of cleanliness. If an examination reveals that the body or clothing of any pupil is "infested with vermin or in a foul condition", the authority may serve a notice on the parent or young person requiring appropriate cleansing to take place. The notice must require that to be done within 24 hours of service. If it is not done to the satisfaction of the medical officer, then he may issue an order requiring the cleansing to be done. In terms of the order, an authority may take the person to a place where the cleansing is to be done and detain him there until it has been completed. The premises, equipment and staff involved must be suitable for the task. A female pupil may only be examined or cleansed by a woman or by a doctor.

If a medical officer has reason to believe that such an exam- **16–11** ination or cleansing is necessary, but that action cannot immediately be taken, he must advise the authority. The authority may then, in the interest of the pupil or other pupils at the school, exclude the pupil from school until the examination or cleansing has taken place.

If the pupil is subsequently found to have again become **16–12** infested with vermin or to be in a foul condition whilst still attending school, due to his own or his parents' neglect, then prosecution may result.[7]

---

[6] The Schools General (Scotland) Regulations 1975 (S.I. 1975 No. 1135), reg. 6.
[7] Education (Scotland) Act 1980, s. 58.

Medical and dental inspection

16–13 In relation to medical and dental treatment of pupils, the Secretary of State plays a leading role as well as the education authority. He must make sure that there are such comprehensive facilities as are necessary to ensure that free medical and dental treatment is available for school children. Education authorities also have a duty in this area. It is to make arrangements to encourage and help school children to take advantage of the medical and dental treatment made available. Parents can, however, say that their children should not be so encouraged by the education authority and if that happens, the authority must abide by the parents' decision.

16–14 In addition, authorities must provide proper facilities for the medical inspection, supervision and treatment referred to. They used to have to provide dental facilities also, but that is no longer required. In cases where the duty of the Secretary of State applies, education authorities can require parents of children attending one of their schools to submit the child to medical or dental inspection in terms of arrangements made by them with the local health board. Failure to comply with any such requirement of the education authority without reasonable excuse is an offence.[8]

Psychological service

16–15 The needs of children in school are many and varied. One of the ways in which education authorities must seek to meet those needs is through the provision of a psychological service. Amongst the functions which that service requires to perform are:

(a) The study of children with special educational needs.

(b) Giving advice to parents and teachers as to appropriate methods of teaching for such children.

(c) Where appropriate, providing for the special educational needs of such children in clinics.

(d) Giving advice to the social work authority regarding the

---

[8] Education (Scotland) Act 1980, s. 57 and National Health Service (Scotland) Act 1978, s. 39.

assessment of the needs of any child for any purpose required by law.[9]

These are the tasks which the law specifically lays down, but the role of the service is not confined to dealing only with children with special educational needs. It can be drawn upon to assist any child who would benefit from it. 16–16

Insurance of Pupils

Education authorities are not required to carry insurance against any of the risks to which pupils may be open whilst in their care. Some schools do sell accident insurance to parents for their children, with the commission usually going to the school fund, but there is no obligation to sell it or for parents to buy it. That is not to say that authorities have no responsibility for accidents to children which occur due to their negligence. They have, and the extent of their liability will vary according to the extent of the injury and any contributory action by the child, taking into account his age and understanding. If authorities do not carry their own insurance, then they will have to bear the cost of any damages from their own funds. 16–17

School Trips

A properly-rounded education cannot, it is suggested, be gained only in the classroom. School trips to, *e.g.* country parks, museums, etc., are a proper and accepted part of school life. Just as they must take reasonable care for the children in their care whilst in school, education authorities must be vigilant for the safety of pupils on school trips. The question of transport has been dealt with, in this context, partly in Chapter 7. Parents and teachers themselves may provide transport for school trips and in such an event, authorities should first ensure that they hold appropriate insurance. 16–18

---

[9] Education (Scotland) Act 1980, s. 4 as amended by the Disabled Persons (Services, Consultation and Representation) Act 1986, s. 14(2).

It may be important to make sure that pupils are suitably clothed for the type of trip they are undertaking. For instance, normal school clothing may be appropriate for a visit to the zoo, but much sturdier clothing would be needed for a nature-study trip in the hills. In the latter case, authorities should ensure that each child has suitable clothing before they set out. Authorities will normally have guidelines on such matters. Similarly, guidelines should be expected to cover the number of adults to children who should be in attendance on school trips. This will probably vary depending on both the nature of the trip and the age of the children. The ratio may also allow for a mixture of adult males/females if this is relevant to the matter.

16–19   Recent events at outdoor centres have given everyone involved some concerns about the safety of children attending them. The Secretary of State issued guidelines for authorities to follow covering such matters as reconnaissance, staffing, safety, insurance, etc., in 1994. The Activity Centres (Young Persons' Safety) Bill which received Royal Assent on June 28, 1995 will allow for the future regulation of facilities where adventure activities are provided.

Extra-curricular Activities

16–20   In many schools, the opportunities provided for children do not stop when the bell goes in the afternoon. Teachers often make themselves available to pupils after school to supervise sports practice, take a drama class, chess club, etc. Provided that any such activity is authorised by the education authority (and the member of staff concerned conducts the activity in accordance with any guidelines laid down by it), then the authority would be liable in the event of an injury being suffered by a pupil caused by its negligence. This should be contrasted with the situation where, *e.g.* a physical education teacher, of his own volition and without any approval from the authority, offers to coach children in his own time as a private individual. In such a case, if a child was injured owing to his negligence, then the teacher would be personally liable, not the authority.

CHAPTER 17

INSPECTION OF SCHOOLS

In many areas there will be regular but informal school visits **17–01** by the authority's councillors and officials who have an interest to check that their schools are functioning effectively and efficiently. In addition, there are the formal inspections of schools carried out by Her Majesty's Inspectors of Schools. These are people appointed by the Secretary of State and are completely independent of education authorities. Their function is to inspect and report on individual nursery, primary and secondary schools. They are concerned with the quality of education provided, the standards being attained and the question of quality and value for money in the schools. In addition they produce general reports on specific areas of education, give advice to the Secretary of State and ensure that new initiatives in the field of education are implemented effectively.

The principal aim of school inspectors is to provide a com- **17–02** prehensive and up-to-date picture of the quality of education being provided throughout the country. This reflects the statement in the Parents' Charter that: "HM Inspectors of Schools assess both the standards schools achieve and the authorities' procedures for assuring quality. Their reports say clearly how well· pupils and schools are doing. They identify good practices, assess value for money and say what schools and authorities must do when their performance is not good enough".[1]

The schools to be inspected in a particular year will be **17–03** chosen as a sample representative of the overall Scottish system of education. Initially, the Inspectors will examine matters relevant to the school as a whole and thereafter they will look in detail at the quality of teaching and learning and the standards of attainment both in the classroom and in national

[1] *The Parents' Charter in Scotland*, Scottish Office 1995, p. 14.

examinations. As part of this process, classes are visited and the quality of teaching is observed. Groups of pupils and staff are interviewed and work is examined. In addition, the Inspectors consider the work of the guidance system and investigate the provision made for pupils with learning difficulties and special educational needs. The management of the school also comes under scrutiny, as does the quality of the accommodation and the resources available within the school.

17–04   During the course of the inspection, findings will be discussed with the headteacher and other appropriate members of staff, but the views of parents and the wider community are also sought. To achieve this, the inspection team will include a "lay" person who is not directly involved in education. Further, in line with the Parents' Charter, parents are involved in the inspection process: "Before and during an inspection, the Inspectors will ask for your views as well as having discussions with the School Board. After the inspection, you will get a summary inspection report from the school showing its strengths, weaknesses and the Inspectors' recommendations."[2] Accordingly, the Inspectors meet with the School Board at the beginning of the inspection process and the views of parents are sought by means of a questionnaire issued to a representative sample of parents. In the case of secondary schools, the Local Enterprise Company and Chamber of Commerce will be informed of the intention to hold the inspection and their views invited.[3]

17–05   At the end of the inspection, a full report is prepared giving the Inspectors' evaluation of the work of the school under three main headings: standards of attainment, the effectiveness of the school, and management and quality assurance. Before the report is finalised, the Inspectors will discuss the provisional conclusions in confidence with the headteacher, the Director of Education and the chairperson of the School Board. When the final report is published, a summary of it is issued to parents, although the full report is available

---

[2] *ibid.*
[3] Scottish Office Education Department Circular 11/93, para. 2.

to them free of charge on request from the local office of HM Inspectors of Schools.[4]

Following the inspection, the school and the education 17–06 authority publish a paper explaining how the recommendations noted in the report are to be implemented. A year later, there will be a further inspection to assess and confirm progress. If the Inspectors are not satisfied, then the school and the education authority will be required to take further action. Again, parents receive a copy of the follow-up report.

As well as inspecting institutions, HM Inspectors also exam- 17–07 ine particular aspects of education. Schools will be visited to gather information for the publication of reports on these matters. Thus, for example, a report could be published concerning the teaching of mathematics in primary schools. These reports are available for purchase from HMSO bookshops.

Again in line with the Parents' Charter, a new audit unit has 17–08 been set up within HM Inspectorate. Its role was described[5] as "to collect, analyse and publish evidence about how well schools and education authorities are performing." Accordingly, the unit is concerned to examine all aspects of effectiveness in education. This includes diverse areas such as methods of assessing examination results, factors such as morale, discipline and guidance; parental consultation; and the management of staff and resources.

---

[4] Circular 11/93 para. 3(vii).
[5] *The Parents' Charter in Scotland*, p. 14.

CHAPTER 18

COMPLAINTS

18–01 Children attend school for at least 11 years. It would be, to say the least, surprising if every child passed through those years without either him, or his parents, having some cause for complaint, however good the schools which they attend are. There are various avenues open to someone who has a complaint, depending upon what it is. A list might read as follows:

(a) The class teacher.

(b) The headteacher.

(c) The Director of Education or other chief education officer.

(d) The Chief Executive of the council.

(e) The parent/teacher association.

(f) The school board.

(g) The councillor for the area in which the school is situated.

(h) The council's internal complaints procedure (if it has one).

(i) The police.

(j) The Commissioner for Local Administration in Scotland (the local ombudsman).

(k) The General Teaching Council for Scotland.

(l) The Secretary of State for Scotland.

18–02 In the face of all of these different people/bodies to whom complaints may be made, it might not be thought surprising if teachers simply could not bear to come to school at all! Authorities should take the attitude, however, that they welcome complaints, not because they operate in a culture of blame, but because they should want to know where they are failing to meet the needs of their customers, the pupils and parents. That is not to say that every complaint will be justified. They manifestly will not, but even an unjustified complaint may highlight an area where a service may be able to be improved and, by so doing, prevent cause for complaint in the future.

It is difficult to give guidance on where the process of **18–03** making a complaint should begin. It depends very much upon what the complaint is. For example, if a child is being bullied, then the class teacher would be the first person to speak to. If no satisfaction were to be obtained, then the headteacher should be approached and then on to the Director of Education and the Chief Executive. Alternatively, the school board or the parent/teacher association might be approached after the headteacher. Schools are under the control of the council and so it is always in order to speak to the local councillor. It is suggested, however, that before doing so, the school should be given the opportunity to deal with a complaint.

Some complaints may be so serious that the police should **18–04** be involved. For instance, if a teacher were to be seen assaulting a pupil, then a parent would be quite justified in reporting the matter to the police. Of course, the school should also be told, as it would wish to consider suspending the teacher pending investigation. Such a serious step should only be taken after the most careful consideration of the matter.

In a case such as assault, the General Teaching Council **18–05** for Scotland might also be approached as it could, if the allegation were to be proven, take away the teacher's registration which is needed to be able to teach. It should be remembered that if a person is not registered with the General Teaching Council, then they are not allowed to teach. It is a body quite independent of councils and could itself stop a person teaching even if a council did not think it appropriate to do so. The grounds upon which the Teaching Council can take such action are if a teacher has been convicted of a serious offence or has otherwise been guilty of professional misconduct.[1]

The Commissioner for Local Administration in Scotland may **18–06** be approached if maladministration is alleged. His advice though is always to complain in writing to the council's Chief Executive before approaching him. The term, maladministration, covers such things as unfair discrimination, incompetence, muddle, delay and failure to follow the authority's own

[1] Teaching Council (Scotland) Act 1965, ss. 10 and 11.

policy or procedures. It covers the way in which a decision is taken but not the decision itself.[2] What the local ombudsman will do is contact the council about the complaint and ask for an explanation if the complaint falls within his remit. He may decide not to investigate the complaint formally and if that is the case, the complainer will be told why. If he decides to investigate formally, then both parties will be told. He will interview relevant people and look at the council's files. If he finds that there has been maladministration, he does not have power to compel an authority to change its procedures which gave rise to the complaint, nor to require compensation to be paid to a successful complainer. It would be rare, however, for an authority to ignore a finding against it and it would be the norm for it to take steps to implement any recommendations in the finding. One of the things which he cannot investigate is a complaint about giving instruction or the internal organisation of schools. This does not bar access to him for everything that might happen in the course of a child's education and, in any event, his advice is – if in doubt, send in the complaint!

18–07   In extremely serious cases, a complaint may be made to the Secretary of State for Scotland about the conduct of a council or of a school board. That may be done where either body is alleged to have failed to carry out any statutory duty laid upon it relating to education.[3] It is worth remembering that a school board has duties quite independent of the council to which its school belongs and care should be taken to identify which body it is that is being complained of.

18–08   If the complaint is found to be justified, then the Secretary of State may make an order declaring the council/school board to be in default of its duty and requiring it to discharge the duty by a given date. If the duty is still not carried out, then he may arrange for the duty to be carried out and recover the cost of so doing from the body in default. Alternatively, he

---

[2] "Call in the Referee", leaflet produced by the Commissioner (Ombudsman) for Local Administration in Scotland, 23 Walker Street, Edinburgh EH5 7HX (tel. 0131-225 5300).
[3] Education (Scotland) Act 1980, s. 70 as amended by the School Boards (Scotland) Act 1988, Sched. 4, para. 6.

may, through the Lord Advocate, ask the Court of Session to order specific performance of the duty. Failure to comply with a decree of the court would render the council/school board in contempt and liable to punishment.

Not all of the things which councils do are duties, *i.e.* things **18–09** which they must do. For example, they must provide primary education. Failure to do so would certainly be a matter for the Secretary of State. On the other hand, councils only have a power to provide nursery education and failure to provide any at all would not enable the Secretary of State to use his power to intervene. Before making a complaint to him, therefore, it would be wise to have established that there is a duty to do what is allegedly not being done.

CHAPTER 19

CONSULTATION

19–01 There may be occasions when a school will informally consult parents about changes which the staff would like to implement, for example to school uniform or arrangements for parking. Such consultation is to gauge opinion and provide information. Where, however, an education authority propose to make changes in matters affecting local education, there may be a requirement that it publishes or makes available in some way its proposals, consults particular persons and takes any representations they make into account before reaching a decision.[1] It should be noted that such consultation is only essential where proposals of the kind being made have been "prescribed", that is specified by the Secretary of State in regulations.[2] The duty to consult and the way in which consultation is effected is, therefore, regulated by law and is not at the discretion of individual authorities.

Prescribed Proposals

19–02 Some examples of prescribed proposals and the persons to be consulted in connection with them are as follows.

A proposal to discontinue a school or stage of education in any school
19–03 A "stage of education" is defined as "a yearly stage of a primary or secondary course of education or all the nursery classes in a school."[3] If it was proposed to close a school

---

[1] Education (Scotland) Act 1980, s. 22A(1).
[2] Education (Scotland) Act 1980, s. 22A(2).
[3] The Education (Publication and Consultation Etc.) (Scotland) Regulations 1981 (S.I. 1981 No. 1558), reg. 2(1) as amended by S.I. 1987 No. 2076.

completely, or to discontinue sixth-year studies in a particular school, the consultation procedures would come into effect. The persons to be consulted in this connection are laid down in the regulations and are: the parent of every pupil attending the school affected by the proposal; the parent of every child of whose existence the education authority are aware and who would be expected to be in attendance at the school or stage of education to be discontinued within two years from the date of the proposal; the school board; and, if appropriate, the church or denominational body in whose interest the school is conducted.

A proposal to change the site of any school
The persons to be consulted in this instance are the parent **19–04** of every pupil in attendance at the school the site of which is to be changed; the parent of every child known to the authority who would be expected to be in attendance at that school within two years from the date of the proposal; the school board; and any church or denominational body in whose interest the school is conducted.

A proposal to provide a new school
Again consultation would be similar to the above cases but **19–05** would include parents of pupils who, in the event of the proposal being implemented, would be liable to be asked by the authority to change from the school attended prior to that event to another school, in other words, those children who would come within the catchment area of the new school; and the parent of every child attending a primary school who is expected to transfer to secondary education within two years of the date of the proposal and who would, in the event of the proposal being implemented, be expected to transfer to a secondary school, other than that to which he would otherwise have been expected to transfer.[4] Again this refers to children in their last two years of primary school who would be expected to transfer to the new, rather than the existing, school.

---

[4] The Education (Publication and Consultation Etc.) (Scotland) Regulations 1981, Sched. 1, paras. (*a*)–(*c*).

19–06   Similar consultation requirements apply to a range of proposals, from a change in a school's catchment area to a proposal to change a single-sex school into a mixed school. Where a change is proposed, it is necessary to check the regulations to determine whether it amounts to a prescribed change and, if so, who must be consulted. A parent in doubt on such an issue can obtain the necessary information from the school concerned or the education authority.

19–07   An authority may make several proposals, including alternative proposals, relating to a particular school. In this case, a single consultation can be carried out in respect of them all. If after this, the authority decides to implement just one of the alternative proposals, there is no requirement to consult further on that proposal.[5]

19–08   Consultation with parents is generally effected by way of a notification being issued by the education authority to each parent. In this respect, "parent" includes guardian and any person who is liable to maintain or has the actual custody of a child.[6] It may be, therefore, that in some instances, dual notification is required. The notification will include a statement outlining the proposal, or such part of it as affects the parent concerned, and will state where full details of the proposal may be obtained. It will also include an address or addresses to which representations on the proposal may be submitted to the authority and will further specify the period within which those representations must be received. This will be a period of not less than 28 days from the date on which the notification is deemed to have been received by the parent. It is important to note that a notification will be deemed to have been received on the day immediately following the date it was issued. This is the case even if a parent can prove that it was received at a later date.[7]

19–09   The notification will also state, if appropriate, the date, time and place of any meeting to be arranged by the authority for the purpose of explaining the proposals and listening to par-

---

[5] S.I. 1987 No. 1558, reg. 5(1B).
[6] Education (Scotland) Act 1980, s. 135(1).
[7] The Education (Publication and Consultation Etc.) (Scotland) Regulations 1981, reg. 5(2)(a) and (b) as amended.

ents' representations. If such a meeting is arranged, it must be held outwith normal working hours and at a place convenient for the parents who would be expected to attend. It must be held not less than 14 days after the date on which the notification is deemed to have been received by the parent. As above, this is the day after the date the notification is issued.[8] The notification can be issued by post or by hand to each parent who needs to be consulted. If that parent has a child attending an education authority school, then the authority may arrange for the notification to be handed to the child for delivery to the parent.[9] Such delivery, however, may be inadequate if the child's parents live separately.

In some instances, for example where it is proposed to dis- **19–10** continue a school or change a catchment area, some of the parents to be consulted will have children who are not yet of school age. In this event, consultation may take the form of an advertisement in a local newspaper which circulates in the district where the school affected is situated. The advertisement must include the details required for personal consultation as outlined above. Similarly, in relation to such a parent, notification shall be deemed to have been received by him on the day immediately following the date of the advertisement.

As regards consultation with the school board, the educa- **19–11** tion authority must give to the clerk of the school board full details of the proposal and request him to submit the board's written representations within a specified period, being not less than 28 days.[10] Similar provisions apply where the authority is required to consult with a church or denominational body.[11]

It will be seen in Chapter 20 that an education authority has **19–12** the power to delegate some of its functions in relation to a school to the school board. It cannot, however, delegate: the function of discontinuing, changing the site of, or amalgamating a school; or the function of setting up or discontinuing any

---

[8] The Education (Publication and Consultation Etc.) (Scotland) Regulations 1981, reg. 5(2)(*b*) and (3).
[9] S.I. 1987 No. 1558, reg. 5(4) and (5).
[10] S.I. 1987 No. 1558, reg. 5(6) and (7).
[11] S.I. 1987 No. 1558, reg. 7.

stage of education in a school, or special classes in a school.[12] In these matters, the school board will simply be consulted as above. It is possible, however, that in relation to other proposals, the function of consultation could be delegated to the board.

19–13   Having completed the necessary consultation procedures, the education authority must take into account all representations received before reaching its decision on the proposal. It must also have regard to the general principle that, so far as is compatible with the provision of suitable instruction and training and the avoidance of unreasonable public expenditure, pupils are to be educated in accordance with the wishes of their parents.[13]

19–14   When proposing to make changes in educational matters the authority, in addition to carrying out the necessary consultation, may be required to submit the proposal to the Secretary of State for his consent. In this case, the proposal cannot be implemented unless than consent is given. Again, the proposals to which this condition applies are "prescribed", being set out in legal regulations. They are:

"(1) proposals to discontinue any school other than a nursery school or any stage of education in a school, other than all the nursery classes in a school, where the change would result in any child at that school (a) if the school is a primary school, having to attend a different primary school at a distance of five miles or more from the original school, the distance being measured by the nearest available route; or (b) where the school is a secondary school, having to attend a different secondary school at a distance of ten miles or more from the school, measured by the nearest available route.

(2) proposals to change the site of any school, other than a nursery school, which would result, in the case of a primary school, in the new site being more than five miles distant from the previous site; and in the case of a secondary school, in the new site being more than ten miles distant from the previous site, measured by the nearest available route.

---

[12] School Boards (Scotland) Act 1988, s. 15(2).
[13] Education (Scotland) Act 1980, s. 28(1); *Harvey v. Strathclyde Regional Council*, 1989 S.L.T. 612 (H.L.).

(3) proposals to discontinue any school or any stage of school education in any school or to change the site of any school or to vary the catchment area of any school, where the number of pupils in attendance at any such school is greater than 80 per cent of that school's capacity. In calculating the pupil capacity, regard must be had to (a) the assessment of capacity on which the authority have based their proposal; (b) the maximum number of pupils in attendance at the school in any one year in the period of ten years preceding the proposal; and (c) the curriculum of the school."[14]

In many instances, the education authority will need to carry out formal consultation as laid down and, in addition, to obtain the consent of the Secretary of State. In such cases, the consultation will be completed before the proposal is submitted to the Secretary of State.

Denominational Schools

There is an extra matter to consider where certain proposals are made regarding denominational schools. This may arise where there is a proposal to discontinue the school or a part of it; to amalgamate the school or part of it with another school; to change the site of the school; to change the arrangements for admission to the school; or to withdraw conditions relating to the management of denominational schools, such as ensuring that teachers appointed to the school are approved as to their religious belief and character. **19–15**

If, following such a proposal, written representations are made by a person authorised by the particular church or religious body concerned and the Secretary of State, having consulted any authority affected by it, is satisfied that the proposal, if implemented, would lead to certain results and that the authority submitting the proposal and the relevant denominational body have failed to reach agreement about it, then the proposal cannot be implemented without his consent. **19–16**

The results referred to are: **19–17**

---

[14] The Education (Publication and Consultation Etc.) (Scotland) Regulations 1981, Sched. 2 as amended.

(a) A significant deterioration for pupils belonging to the area of the authority submitting the proposal.

(b) A significant deterioration for pupils from any other authority.

(c) Such deterioration for pupils at (a) above and pupils belonging to the area of another authority, which, taken together, amounts to a significant deterioration in the provision, distribution or availability of education in denominational schools compared with such provision, distribution or availability in other public schools.

19–18   In such a situation, the Secretary of State's consent will not be granted unless he is satisfied that adequate arrangements have been made for the religious instruction of the children who will no longer be educated in a denominational school. In granting consent, the Secretary of State may impose such conditions as he sees fit with regard to the religious instruction of the children affected and to other related matters. Any of these conditions may be revoked or amended by him at any time.

19–19   Any question which may arise as to whether a particular proposal is one to which these provisions apply, as to the implementation of a proposal to which the Secretary of State has consented, or as to the fulfilment or observation of any conditions imposed by him when he gave consent, will be determined by the Secretary of State himself. The education authority must perform its duties in this respect in accordance with any such determination.[15]

19–20   Certain types of proposal for which consultation is required can be "frozen" if a school board commences the procedure for the acquisition of self-governing status. For further details, see Chapter 21.

[15] Education (Scotland) Act 1980, s. 22D as amended by the Local Government etc. (Scotland) Act 1994, s. 144.

CHAPTER 20

SCHOOL BOARDS

Introduction

School boards were introduced comparatively recently into   **20–01**
the Scottish educational scene, the first ones being formed in
1989. They can only be formed in public schools and give to
board members the opportunity to be consulted on certain
matters relating to the running of schools and, on other matters, to take quite important decisions. They are not controlled
by councils, although they may be assisted by them in carrying out their tasks. In the areas where they have responsibilities, they make their own decisions and are not generally
bound by the policies of the council which owns the schools
for which they have been formed. They are established when
the required number of parent members have been elected.
It is not necessary for there to have been staff members
elected for a board to be established.[1]

Funding of Boards

School boards are funded by the council in whose area they   **20–02**
are situated. Before the start of each financial year (April 1),
councils must consult with each board as to the amount of
money they require to meet their administrative and training
expenses, other outgoings and generally the expenses of carrying out the functions which the law has given them. Their
allocation must be set by councils before the start of each
financial year. The money is then made available to each
board as it needs it and, indeed, more money than originally
allocated may be made available if it is thought appropriate.

---

[1] School Boards (Scotland) Act 1988, s. 1(4).

Boards may not get all that they ask for. Councils only have to give what they think is reasonably required. They must also supply to boards information which has been prescribed about revenue and capital expenditure which has been expended on the school in the previous financial year and what is proposed to be spent in the financial year in which the information about the previous year is given.[2]

Membership of Boards

20–03 There are three different types of member of a school board – parent, staff and co-opted. Parent members form the largest section of the membership. Any parent of a pupil in attendance at a school may be elected to a school board by other parents of pupils in attendance. The term "parent" does not mean only the natural parent of a child. It also means any other natural person who is his guardian, who has custody of him or who is liable to maintain him. So, for example, if a child's parents were dead and his grandparents had custody of him, for this purpose, they would be his "parents" and could stand and vote in school board elections.[3] Members of staff who have children at the same school cannot stand as parent members although they can vote in parent elections.[4]

20–04   The staff of a school are also entitled to elect one or more of their number to be a member of a school board. Not everyone employed in a school is covered by the term "staff", however. What the word means is teachers and instructors, whether full-time or part-time, employed by the authority for the purpose of providing education at that school, whether or not they are also so employed at other schools. So, for example, a visiting music instructor would be eligible to stand and vote in staff elections at any of the schools in which he gives instruction. The term clearly does not include janitors or school secretar-

---

[2] School Boards (Scotland) Act 1988, s. 17.
[3] School Boards (Scotland) Act 1988, s. 2(1) and s. 22(2).
[4] School Boards (Scotland) Act 1988, s. 2(4) and Sched. 1, para. 4; but see s. 2(6).

ies as they are not employed to provide education at the school. Headteachers are not eligible to stand for election or to vote.[5] They do, however, have the right to attend, speak and give advice at board meetings. If a board so decides, a headteacher must give advice to it on any matter within a board's competence.[6]

The final category of member is the co-opted member. **20–05** Such persons are chosen by the other board members as soon as is practicable after the establishment of the board. Neither parents nor staff who are eligible for election can be co-opted to a board.[7] If the school is a denominational school, then one of the co-opted members must be a person nominated by the church or denominational body in whose interest the school is conducted.[8] It is, however, open to a board to decline to accept a particular nomination. There is no requirement for parent or staff members of the board of a denominational school to belong to that particular denomination. It is also possible to co-opt a young person – that is someone who has reached 16 years of age but has not yet attained 18 years of age.[9] There is no bar to such a person being a pupil at the same school.

Size of Boards

Not all boards are of the same size. The number of pupils at **20–06** a school determines the size of a board. Clearly the number of pupils will vary and so the determining number is the number of pupils at the school on August 31 preceding the board's first establishment and on the same date preceding each biennial election of parent members. This table[10] shows the respective composition of boards depending upon four different school sizes:

---

[5] School Boards (Scotland) Act 1988, s. 2(1)(b) and (13).
[6] School Boards (Scotland) Act 1988, s. 5(3).
[7] School Boards (Scotland) Act 1988, s. 2(5) and (10).
[8] School Boards (Scotland) Act 1988, s. 2(7).
[9] School Boards (Scotland) Act 1988, s. 4(2).
[10] School Boards (Scotland) Regulations 1989 (S.I. 1989 No. 273), reg. 4(1).

PUPILS	PARENT MEMBERS	STAFF MEMBERS	CO-OPTED MEMBERS
1–500	4	1	2
501–1,000	5	2	2
1,001–1,500	6	2	3
over 1,500	7	3	3

Expenses of Board Members

20–07   Travel and subsistence allowances are payable by councils to board members for attending board meetings or for any other matter related to the functions of a board which has been approved by the council. The level of the allowances is tied to those payable to members of councils. They can be up to the same as those paid to council members, but cannot exceed them.[11]

Term of Office of Members

20–08   Although the normal term of office of a board member is four years, when a board is first formed, half of the parent members must retire after two years. There are, therefore, elections to each board every two years. The parent members themselves decide who is to resign after two years. If they cannot agree, then the decision must be made by lot. If a casual vacancy arises for a parent or staff member, then a by-election must be held within three months, unless there is less than six months of the term of office to run. If a vacancy for a co-opted member occurs, then another person must be co-opted. Members filling a casual vacancy serve the remainder of the term of office of the person whose vacancy they have filled.[12]

---

[11] School Boards (Scotland) Act 1988, s. 19.
[12] School Boards (Scotland) Act 1988, s. 3.

Posts of Chairman and Vice-chairman

A board must elect a chairman and a vice-chairman from its **20-09** parent or co-opted members. Staff members are not eligible for either post. The chairman has a casting vote in all matters except those relating to the appointment of a co-opted member and the appointment to any particular office or committee. In such cases, the decision must be made by lot in the event of equality of voting. In the absence of the chairman, the vice-chairman has the casting vote.[13]

Disqualification from Membership

Not everyone who would otherwise be entitled to be a board **20-10** member can in fact be one. Some people are disqualified. They are: (a) a person disqualified from being nominated as a candidate, or being elected, or from being a member of a council by reason of bankruptcy or conviction of a criminal offence resulting in a sentence of imprisonment passed within the previous five years; and (b) a person subject to legal incapacity, but excepting a young person who may be co-opted to the board as stated above.

It should also be noted that, although the Director of Educa- **20-11** tion, or any of his nominated education officers, is entitled to attend and speak at any meeting of a school board in the authority's area, he shall not be a member of that board and thus will not have voting rights. Similarly, the elected councillor for the area in which a school is situated is entitled to attend and speak at any meeting of the school board, but will not be a member of the board.[14]

In addition to these restrictions, a current board member **20-12** may be removed from office by a board if it is satisfied that he is unable to carry out his duties by reason of physical or mental illness or incapacity. A member may also be removed if he has failed without good cause to attend meetings for a

---

[13] School Boards (Scotland) Act 1988, s. 6(1) and (2).
[14] School Boards (Scotland) Act 1988, ss. 4 and 5.

continuous period of at least six months and to attend three consecutive meetings.[15]

School Board Clerks

20–13   Every board must appoint a clerk. The clerk need not be a member of the board. Payment can be made to the clerk, but only if he is not a member of the board.[16]

Meetings of Boards

20–14   There are no requirements as to the procedures which boards must follow in their meetings. They have the power to regulate their own proceedings whilst abiding by the terms of the School Boards (Scotland) Act 1988. There must be a quorum at meetings, however, and the requirement is that not less than one-third of their members must be present. Boards' proceedings are not to be held invalid because a vacancy has yet to be filled or because of a defect in the qualifications, election, or co-option of any member although, if any such defect subsequently came to light, then the affected person should cease to attend meetings and his place should be filled in the appropriate way.[17]

20–15   A copy of the agenda for each board meeting must be made available at the school for anyone who wishes to see it, together with the draft minutes of the last meeting once approved by the chairman, the minutes approved by the board and any report or document considered at a meeting. There is no minimum time laid down between the issue of an agenda and the meeting of the board which it calls. Boards should have adopted their own standing orders which cover such matters. There are some documents which need not be made available. They are documents which relate to:

[15] School Boards (Scotland) Act 1988, s. 3(5).
[16] School Boards (Scotland) Act 1988, s. 6(10).
[17] School Boards (Scotland) Act 1988, ss. 6(5)–(7).

(a) A particular person employed at, formerly employed at, or who has applied to be employed at, the school.
(b) A particular person who is, has been, or is likely to be, a pupil at the school.
(c) Any information which the board is legally obliged not to disclose.
(d) Any matter which the board is satisfied should be dealt with on a confidential basis because of its nature.

Anyone may attend a board meeting but a board may exclude the public from a meeting when considering any matter covered in (a) to (d).[18]

Minutes of meetings are to be taken and signed at the same **20–16** or the subsequent meeting by the then chairman. If required by the council, a copy of the minutes must be sent to it.

Boards may form committees to consider and report on **20–17** matters referred to them. They can only make recommendations to the board and not take decisions themselves. If a board so wishes, it can include in the membership of a committee a number of persons, up to half, who are not board members.[19]

Signing/Service of Documents

Sometimes documents will have to be signed on behalf of a **20–18** board and boards can authorise any of their members or their clerks to do that for them. Any documents which have to be served on a board should be served on the clerk or, if there is none, on the chairman or vice-chairman.[20]

FUNCTIONS OF A BOARD

School boards have a number of different powers and duties, **20–19** ranging from influencing the appointment of senior staff in the

---

[18] Schools Boards (Scotland) Regulations 1989 (S.I. 1989 No. 273), regs. 8(1) and (2) and 9(1) and (2).
[19] School Boards (Scotland) Act 1988, s. 6(3), (7) and (8).
[20] School Boards (Scotland) Act 1988, s. 6(4).

school to having the right to be provided with certain financial information. These are next considered in detail.

Control over Spending

20–20 Councils must make available to headteachers such funds as they think necessary for the purchase of books, teaching materials for the school and such other purposes as they think fit. The headteacher cannot simply spend money as he wishes. He must make proposals to the board as to how it should be spent and must obtain the board's approval for his plans. If the board does not approve the proposals, the money cannot be spent. There is no mechanism for resolving a situation where neither board nor headteacher will alter their position! Both must have regard to any guidance issued by the council in such matters and any of its policies in relation to the curriculum. They must also ensure that any relevant duty of the council under statute or any rule of law is complied with.[21]

The Right to Information

20–21 A board has the general right to be supplied with information about its school and the provision of education in the area covered by its council. When it is first established it must be provided with policy statements about school rules, discipline, uniform, the assessment of pupils and the curriculum by the headteacher. Any changes in these must be notified to the board by the headteacher. He must supply an annual report to the board covering, amongst other things, information on the level of attainment of pupils in the school. It should be noted that the right of the board is to be told of these things and not to control them. A board may, however, comment on such matters to the headteacher and the council and account must be taken of what boards say and replies given. A board

---

[21] School Boards (Scotland) Act 1988, s. 9.

may also require reports and information about the school and these must be provided, if reasonable.[22]

Relations with Parents and the Community

School boards are required to interact not only with the educa- **20–22** tion authorities, but with the community as a whole. There is a duty laid upon them to promote contact between the school, parents and the community. They are required to try to secure the formation of parent/teacher or parents' associations. They are also made in some way accountable to parents by having to report to them at least once a year on what they have done and to find out what parents think about matters for which they are responsible. Headteachers must help them in this by telling them what means there are already for consultation between parents and teachers. Again, boards may comment on them to the headteacher and he must consider any such comments and reply to them. Members of the public may attend school board meetings and can only be excluded for items of business which are confidential.

There may be occasions when there is a matter of such **20–23** importance that parents wish to address the board and make their views known outwith the reporting meeting referred to above. If enough parents so request in writing, then the board must hold a meeting for parents. The number of signatures needed is 30 parents of pupils in attendance at the school or at least a quarter of those entitled to vote at the most recently-held election of parent members, whichever is the less. Such a meeting can only be called to make inquiries and to discuss matters relating to the activities of the board and to make res-olutions relating to those activities. A request for such a meet-ing must give notice of the purpose of the meeting, the matters to be raised or the resolutions to be proposed. Boards are not, however, bound by any resolutions made. When a board receives such a notice, it must set as early as possible a date for the meeting but must, in so doing, have regard to the desir-ability of giving all parents due notice. So it would not, it is

---

[22] School Boards (Scotland) Act 1988, s. 10.

thought, be good practice to give notice of a meeting in the middle of the Easter holidays when a large number of parents would be likely to be on holiday. Parents must be told where and when the meeting is to be held, for what purpose and what resolutions have been given notice of. The board must decide which of its members are to attend and who will chair the meeting. The headteacher may attend and speak, as may any other person invited to come by the board. Parents, of course, may speak also. Members of the council and its officers are not entitled to attend unless invited by the board. Only parents can vote, not invited persons.[23]

Control of School Premises

20–24   School boards have a duty to control the use of school premises outwith school hours. The term "school premises" covers not only the buildings, but the playing fields as well and any accommodation where pupils are boarded. So, if the local badminton club wishes to use the school gymnasium in the evening, it must first obtain the permission of the school board. Not only do boards control the use of the premises, they have a duty laid upon them to encourage the use of the premises by the local community. All of this is subject to the power of the council to make directions as to the exercise of such control and to the council's right to fix the level of charges.[24]

Local Holidays

20–25   Whilst councils retain the right to decide what the main session (term) arrangements for schools are, school boards have the power to fix occasional holidays during the school term after consulting with their councils. In practice, councils have to decide how many holidays boards can set, as the number of days on which pupils must attend school is regulated by

[23] School Boards (Scotland) Act 1988, s. 13.
[24] School Boards (Scotland) Act 1988, s. 14(1).

law and it would be impossible for boards to set as many holidays as they liked.[25]

Fundraising

School boards have the power to raise money by any means **20–26** other than borrowing and to receive gifts, although they cannot acquire any interest in heritable property which, broadly, covers land and buildings. They can spend anything so raised or received for the benefit of the school. Although boards must take account of the views of the headteacher in reaching their decisions, they have the freedom to spend the money as they think will benefit the school. The headteacher does not have the same right of veto over a board's spending plan as a board has over a headteacher's! If a board is disestablished, any property passes to the council to be used for the benefit of the school. If the board is re-established, then any property left passes back to the control of the new board.[26]

Devolved School Management

The Secretary of State, in circular 6/93, invited education **20–27** authorities to bring forward schemes of devolved school management for all of their schools (apart from nursery schools) against a set timetable. The circular sets out the framework within which schemes should work. Schemes for each authority are likely to be different but there are a number of ways in which they should all affect school boards. Schemes should allow for decisions at school level to be taken by headteachers after consultation with their school boards. Authorities should monitor the effectiveness of schemes in consultation with boards, amongst other interested parties. Schemes should allow for the delegation of 80 per cent of school-level expenditure either to headteachers or to school boards under the normal delegation rules. Boards should also have a consultative role on the vary-

---

[25] School Boards (Scotland) Act 1988, s. 14(2).
[26] School Boards (Scotland) Act 1988, s. 18.

ing of staffing levels, subject to minimum standards being maintained and, if boards so desire, for the involvement of board members and nominees of the authority in the selection of staff.[27] School boards should be consulted in the preparation of school development plans and a copy of the agreed plan should be made available to each member of a board.[28]

Delegation of Further Powers

20–28 It is possible for school boards to acquire from the authority greater powers than those which the School Boards (Scotland) Act 1988 gave to them. This can be done either by the authority offering them to a board, or at the instigation of a board itself. The formal means by which extra powers are granted is through a "delegation order". This order can delegate powers to a board for a limited period or without a time limit. Conditions may be attached to the delegation of powers. Delegation orders can be amended or revoked. The following matters cannot be delegated, however:
  (a) Employing, dismissing or removing school staff.
  (b) Selecting for appointment someone to be headteacher or deputy or assistant headteacher.
  (c) The regulation of the curriculum.
  (d) The actual assessment of pupils.
  (e) The function of discontinuing, changing the site of, or amalgamating with another school a school (or part of a school).
  (f) The function of setting up or discontinuing any stage of education in a school, or special classes in a school.
  (g) The function of determining admissions policy for a school.[29]

Delegation with the Consent of the Authority

20–29 If an authority wishes to delegate powers to a board, then it must give to it a draft of the order and obtain the board's agree-

---

[27] See appendix 2.
[28] See appendix 3.
[29] School Boards (Scotland) Act 1988, s. 15.

ment to it. If the board does not agree, the order cannot be made. On the other hand, a board may itself approach an authority for extra powers. If the authority agrees to the making of an order (and it must tell the board as soon as is practicable, and in any event within six months), then it must give the board a draft of the order and try to reach agreement on its terms. Once agreement has been reached, then it must make the order forthwith. If agreement cannot be reached within two months of the draft being provided, then the board can ask the authority to send the latest draft to the Secretary of State. He then has to consider the views of the authority and the board. If he thinks that the making of the order would prejudice the good running of the school, he will not require the order to be made. If he does not think that the good running of the school would be prejudiced, then he will direct the authority to make the order in such terms as he considers appropriate.[30]

Delegation Against the Wishes of the Authority

If a board wishes to have powers delegated to it, it must put **20–30** its request to the authority in writing. The request must be considered as soon as is practicable and, in any event, the authority must advise the board of its decision within six months. If it refuses to delegate the powers asked for (and reasons must be given), then, if the board still wishes to proceed, it must call for a ballot of all parents of pupils in attendance at the school. The ballot is carried out by the authority and the normal rules for school board elections apply, with appropriate modifications. Parents must be given a ballot paper to enable them to vote "yes" or "no" to the proposals, a statement of the board's proposals and any reasons given for them, the authority's reasons for refusal and any reply made by the board to them. If a majority of parents vote for the proposals then the authority must consider the matter again. If it refuses a second time, the board may refer the matter to the Secretary of State. Unless, after consulting both parties, he considers that the delegation would prejudice the good run-

---

[30] School Boards (Scotland) Act 1988, s. 15 and Sched. 3, paras. 1 and 9–12.

ning of the school, he will direct the authority to make the delegation order in such terms as he considers appropriate.[31]

Power of Secretary of State to Require Information

20–31 Where the Secretary of State requires further information to help him to reach a decision on any such case referred to him, he may require either party to supply him with same.

Amendment/Revocation of Delegation Orders

20–32 An order may be amended or revoked in whole or in part by the making of a further order with the consent of the board. If the authority cannot obtain the consent of the board, it may send a draft order to the Secretary of State. He will call for the views of both parties for consideration. If he considers that continued delegation of any function would prejudice the good running of the school, he may consent to the revocation of that function or to an amendment of the delegation. He may direct that alterations be made to the draft order. If the authority then decides to proceed with the draft order, it must follow his directions.[32]

Appointment Committees

20–33 Where a school has a school board, it has a significant input to the appointment of a new headteacher, deputy headteacher and assistant headteacher(s). Ultimately, the decision is made by the authority on the recommendation of the appointment committee but, unless the committee considers that no one is suitable for the post, its recommendation must be accepted unless the candidate is ineligible for it, for example if he does

---

[31] School Boards (Scotland) Act 1988, s. 15 and Sched. 3, paras. 3–8.
[32] School Boards (Scotland) Act, Sched. 3, paras. 14 and 15.

not hold the relevant teaching qualification. Leading up to that point is a procedure which must be followed.

To fill such posts other than on an acting basis, the council **20–34** must first advertise them in such publications circulating throughout Scotland as it considers appropriate. The council must then prepare a short leet of applicants. If there are less than four eligible applicants, then the post can either be re-advertised or all of the applicants must be placed on the short leet. If there are more than three eligible applicants either after the initial or a second advertisement, then the short leet must consist of at least three of them.

In the case of the appointment of a headteacher, the short **20–35** leet must be put to the school board to consider. The board can add names to, or delete names from, the leet. Additions can only be made from the names of those who have actually applied for the post and are eligible for it. The leet cannot be reduced to less than three names. If there are only three names or less on the leet in the first place, the board may only make comments on them to the appointment committee which has to take them into consideration. When performing this task, boards must meet without their staff and pupil members (if any). They must also tell the education authority that they are meeting to consider the short leet, as it is entitled to attend and give advice which must be considered. There is a requirement for school board nominees to be members of an appointment committee. The authority decides upon the actual size of the committee. For the appointment of a headteacher, it must be made up of equal numbers of authority nominees and board nominees, the chair being held by an authority nominee. For the appointment of a deputy headteacher or an assistant headteacher, the headteacher takes the chair and the other places are filled by equal numbers of nominees of the authority and the board. The voting procedures of appointment committees are determined by the procedures of the committee's parent authority. Members are entitled to allowances and expenses determined by the Secretary of State.[33]

---

[33] School Boards (Scotland) Act 1988, s. 11 and Sched. 2. See also Chapter 12, para. 12–09 *re* appointment of teachers in denominational schools.

ELECTIONS

20–36 Councils are responsible for making arrangements for the holding of elections to their school boards. They have to draw up what is called a scheme of arrangements for that purpose. Schemes may be different for different schools or types of school. The Secretary of State may issue guidance about the form and content of schemes which councils have to comply with. A returning officer must be appointed by each council to ensure the proper conduct of elections. Councils may direct that school boards themselves should conduct the elections in accordance with any directions which they may give although boards cannot make or vary schemes of arrangements.

Schemes of Arrangements for Elections

20–37 Schemes must be written down and executed by the council. They must contain the main elements of electoral procedure and the main arrangements as to the timing of events and responsibility for discharge of the council's duties for elections and ballots. They must be available for public inspection. Schemes must contain certain information, including the following, although more may be included if appropriate:

(a) The issue of notice of elections or ballots to all parents of pupils in attendance at the school.

(b) The provision of nomination papers, and invitations to candidates to submit a personal statement for circulation to parents with the voting paper (elections only).

(c) Closure of electoral rolls.

(d) Return of nomination papers and statements by candidates (elections only).

(e) Issue of voting papers, personal statements submitted by candidates (elections only), and the statements of proposals and reasons for them to all parents on the roll (ballots only).

(f) Return of completed voting papers.

(g) Counting of votes.

(h) Announcement of results.

(i) Establishment and maintenance of electoral rolls.

(j)   Appointment of a returning officer, his deputies and assistants (where required) and their duties.
(k)   Details of the electoral system.
(l)   Nomination arrangements.

Electoral Rolls

Authorities must maintain electoral rolls, identifying parents of   **20–38**
pupils in attendance at each school and staff. Unless parents' names appear on the roll, they cannot stand or vote in elections. Eligibility to vote or to be a candidate is determined by the authority. Electoral rolls can only be used for the administration of elections and ballots and for no other purpose. Parents and staff may check that they are on the roll and that the entry is correct but otherwise they are totally confidential and can only be accessed by those who keep them up to date or who organise the elections or ballots. This restriction can cause difficulties for parents. It is not unknown for candidates to want to check that their seconder is on the roll but to find that they cannot gain access to that information. It is understood that this restriction was introduced to prevent separated parents from finding out where their partners live. How effective this is is open to doubt because if the authority knows where each parent lives, it must try to ensure that their names are on the electoral roll, thus disclosing the school which their child attends.

Authorities must take all practicable steps to ensure that   **20–39**
every person known to be a parent of a pupil in attendance at a school knows about forthcoming parental elections and that they can both stand and vote and have the opportunity to do so.

Nomination of Candidates

Parents
Schemes may provide that a candidate requires a proposer   **20–40**
and a seconder, but may not specify more than that. Less may be required generally and particularly for the smallest schools.

Staff

20–41 Staff do not need more than a proposer, who must be eligible to vote in the election. Where there are fewer than four eligible staff members, then they may nominate themselves without a proposer.

Elections

20–42 Elections are to be held by secret ballot and every parent of a pupil in attendance at a school must have the opportunity to vote by post. There is no requirement for staff to have that opportunity although it might be appropriate for visiting teachers or for staff who are absent because of illness. Staff who have children at the same school may vote in parental elections and in ballots although they may not stand as parent members. Parents must be sent a ballot paper and, if there are any, copies of candidates' statements if received by such date as may have been set. These statements must not exceed 250 words in length. Authorities may properly ask for them to be amended or refuse to circulate them if they contain defamatory or other material which it would be illegal for councils to distribute otherwise, such as material expressing support for a political party. No other material designed to influence the election may be circulated.

The Count

20–43 The counting of votes in elections may be attended by candidates or their representatives. In the case of ballots, representatives of the authority and the school board may attend.[34]

Disestablishment of School Boards

20–44 A school board must be established before it can be disestablished. It is established when the required number of

---

[34] School Boards (Scotland) Act 1988, Sched. 1 and Scottish Education Department Circular 3/1989.

parent members has been elected. If, at an election, the required number of parents has not been elected, then a by-election must be held as soon as is practicable. If, following the by-election, the required number of parents has not been elected, then either the board cannot be established or, if it had already been established, it must be disestablished. In either event, further elections must be held either within 22 to 24 months of the last election or when a number of parents equal to the number prescribed for the board request it in writing. There is no provision for parents to request that a board be not formed. It is quite possible, therefore, for less than a handful of parents to cause a board to be formed when the majority of parents, through choice or indifference, would have wished the opposite.

On the disestablishment of a board, all of its functions, del- **20–45** egated or otherwise, fall to be exercised by the authority. A re-established board re-assumes all of the former functions of the last board, whether delegated or not. Where a school board has not been established because there are insufficient parents to constitute one and the Secretary of State has consented to that decision, or an existing board has been disestablished, the few parents of pupils in attendance have the right themselves to certain information which would have been available to the school board.[35]

Interim Boards

It sometimes happens that two or more schools are amalgam- **20–46** ated. If they each have boards, then account is taken of that. What then happens is that the boards combine to form what is known as an interim school board made up of all of the members of the existing boards. Even if an existing board would otherwise have been disestablished before a board is formed for a combined school, the remaining members remain members of the interim board but the vacancies in the existing membership cannot be filled. The board for the combined school will be established in the same way as the

---

[35] School Boards (Scotland) Act 1988, s. 20.

board for a new school. Bearing in mind the above, an interim school board has the same powers as an ordinary board. The provisions of the Act relating to the making and suspension of delegation orders do not apply to an interim board. It appears, therefore, that delegation orders cannot be made to an interim board, nor can existing delegation orders be suspended.[36]

[36] School Boards (Scotland) Act 1988, s. 7.

CHAPTER 21

SELF-GOVERNING SCHOOLS

The Scottish system of council-managed school education   **21–01**
has been subject to a large number of changes in the recent
past. The rationale of many of them has been to try to give
more information to parents and, indeed, the general public,
to involve parents more in the way in which the schools which
their children attend are managed and, through devices such
as the publication of performance indicators, to compare certain aspects of the performance of their own authority with
those of authorities in other parts of the country.

Until fairly recently, parents who could not afford a private   **21–02**
education for their children (and who could not educate them
satisfactorily themselves) had little choice but to send them
to a school managed by a local authority. The introduction of
the Self-Governing Schools etc. (Scotland) Act 1989 changed
that. The Act gave parents of children who attend an education-authority managed school the opportunity to take over the
running of the school themselves and remove it from the control of the authority. This is commonly known as "opting out",
although the proper terminology is "the acquisition of self-
governing status". It has to be said that, so far at least, it has
been a very rarely-used power, with only one incidence at the
time of writing of a school opting out. That having been said,
there is no knowing how popular such a move will be in the
future and so it is thought right to deal with the subject,
although in general terms. Parents or a school board considering such a move would be well advised to seek legal
advice in view of the very serious consequences for themselves and the children at the school, not to mention the com-
plexities of the procedure.

Funding of Self-governing Schools

It is the duty of the Secretary of State, not the authority, to fund   **21–03**
self-governing schools. He does this by way of three types

of grant. One covers the normal running costs of the school (recurrent grant). Another covers capital expenditure (capital grant). The third type covers expenditure not of a capital nature which the Secretary of State does not think should be met from recurrent grant (special purpose grant). Regulations set out the criteria for each type of grant. The funding of special schools is also determined by the Secretary of State, but involves discussion with the education authority.[1]

Which Schools are Eligible?

21–04 Basically, any public school which has a school board can acquire self-governing status. There are exceptions to the general rule. They are nursery schools and schools affected by a final decision to close or amalgamate them.[2]

How is Self-governing Status Obtained?

21–05 First of all, the school must have a school board. After that, there are two ways in which the procedure can begin. The board can start it itself by deciding to hold a ballot of parents on the subject. The board must pass a resolution to that effect, but one such resolution is not enough. A second one must be passed not less than 28 days and not more than 42 days after the first one. The other way of beginning is for parents themselves to request that the board hold a ballot on the subject. A certain number of parents is needed to make such a request, the number varying with the size of the school. So for schools with under 60 parents on the electoral roll at the date of the last school board election, a majority is needed. For other schools a minimum of 30 parents is needed and more if 30 is not at least 10 per cent of the school board electoral roll at the date of the last election.

21–06 Each of these steps, the first and second resolutions, and

---

[1] Self-Governing Schools etc. (Scotland) Act 1989, ss. 26 and 27.
[2] Self-Governing Schools etc. (Scotland) Act 1989, s. 13 and Self-Governing Schools (Suspension of Proposals) (Scotland) Order 1994.

the receipt of the parental request must be intimated by the school board to the authority and to the Secretary of State. If the school is denominational, the relevant denominational body must also be advised. Notification is important because of the restrictions which the start of the procedure imposes on councils.[3]

The ballot must be organised (as things stand) by the Elect- **21–07** oral Reform Society and must be a secret postal ballot.[4] After the second resolution by a board has been passed or the parental request for a ballot received, the ballot itself must be held within three months. All parents of pupils in attendance at the school are entitled to vote. The board may require the authority to send to it a copy of the roll which it holds for school board elections to help it in that regard, but the roll may well be incomplete and the board has the responsibility to decide who is eligible to vote. Once the ballot has taken place, the first thing to be done is to check whether 50 per cent of those eligible to vote have in fact voted. If less than 50 per cent voted, the result is of no consequence and a second ballot must be held within 14 days of the day following the first ballot. The school board has a duty to make sure that the body conducting the election gives to voters enough information about the effect of acquiring self-governing status to enable them to form a proper judgment on the question, an explanation of the process, an indication that they are entitled to vote and a ballot paper inviting them to vote either "yes" or "no". The Secretary of State may prescribe a limit on the amount of money which authorities and boards may spend on influencing the outcome of ballots. Boards may recover their expenses from the Secretary of State. A fresh ballot may be ordered by him if the rules have been broken or if a board has acted unreasonably. A simple majority in favour of, or against, the proposal is all that is required.[5]

---

[3] Self-Governing Schools etc. (Scotland) Act 1989, s. 13. See also para. 21–27.
[4] Self-Governing Schools (Ballots and Publication of Proposals) (Scotland) Regulations 1990, reg. 2 and Sched. 3, paras. 1 and 3 of the 1989 Act.
[5] Self-Governing Schools etc. (Scotland) Act 1989, ss. 14 and 15 and Sched. 3. See also 1990 Regulations.

After the Ballot

21–08   If the result is a "no" vote, then that is the end of the matter, although the procedure can be started again at any time. If the vote is a "yes" one, the next stage is for the board to publish its proposals for the acquisition of self-governing status within one month from the date on which the result of the ballot is determined or such longer period as the Secretary of State may permit. The proposals must give the following information:

(a)   The name of the board of management (the new governing body of the school).

(b)   The make-up of membership of the board of management.

(c)   The arrangements for admission of pupils, any special educational emphasis, and such information as to the management of the school as the board thinks fit.

(d)   The date of implementation of the proposals.

(e)   Such other information as may be prescribed.

21–09   This must be accompanied by prescribed information which describes the school as at the date of publication (*e.g.* whether it is a primary or secondary school, a denominational school, etc.) and that the matters described will continue to be "characteristics" of the school should it become self-governing. There must also be included a statement that the school board will become an interim board of management with a board of management taking over within three months thereafter. The board would be comprised, among others, of a majority of elected parent members with elected staff members.

21–10   It may be thought odd that the proposals only need to be published after the ballot. Parents would have a better idea of what they were voting for if they were required to be published before it! Be that as it may, the proposals must be sent to the Secretary of State, the education authority and (if applicable) the denominational body within one month from the date on which the result of the ballot is determined. There then follows a period of two months from the date of publication of the proposals for any person (not just parents) to make representations on them to the Secretary of State. It is important to note that proposals, once published, cannot be withdrawn without the consent of the Secretary of State. He may also impose conditions on allowing a withdrawal. It may be seen, therefore, that the publication of proposals is not a step to be taken lightly as it cannot be guaranteed to be reversed.[6]

Once the Secretary of State has received the proposals, he **21–11** can:

(a) Reject them, having first consulted the board as to the possibility.
(b) Approve them.
(c) Approve them with modifications (after consulting the board and the authority).

Before reaching his decision, he must consider the following:

(a) Any relevant representations.
(b) The percentage of votes cast in the ballot preceding the publication of the proposals.
(c) The percentage of votes cast in favour of self-governing status as against the votes cast.
(d) Such other matters as he considers appropriate.

A board must give the Secretary of State such information **21–12** as he may require of it to enable him to consider his decision. If, during the two months after publication of the proposals, the board should be disestablished, the proposals must be rejected. If the proposals are approved, then the Secretary of State chooses a date when the school is to assume self-governing status, which may be either the date in the proposals or a later date (the incorporation date). On the due date, an interim board of management is formed under the name given in the proposals as a corporate body. On that date, the school board ceases to exist. The members of the school board become, automatically, members of the interim board of management. Being, however, only an "interim" board of management, one of its first tasks is to have elected the board of management. That must be done within three months of the incorporation date. Regardless of the terms left to run as school board members, the members of the school board remain in office as members of the interim board of management until the election of the board of management, at which point the interim board also ceases to exist and the

---

[6] Self-Governing Schools etc. (Scotland) Act 1989, ss. 16 and 18.

board of management takes over. The self-governing school can then be said to have fully acquired its new status. Once the new status has been achieved the council must, either on the incorporation date or as soon as practicable thereafter, provide the board of management with all of the information which it holds in respect of the school, including its administration, the school buildings, the staff transferring and the pupils.[7]

21–13   That, then, is the procedure, but there are a number of consequences brought about by different triggers in the process. What is to become of the staff? How is the school property belonging to the school to be decided upon and transferred? Are all of the ties with the authority severed? What is a board of management and how does it operate? This chapter will continue by dealing with these and other related matters.

Boards of Management

21–14   As the whole object of acquiring self-governing status is for the school to be transferred from the control of the authority, it is perhaps appropriate to begin with describing what it is exactly that takes over the management of the school when the management of the authority is ended. The new governing body is called a board of management and is known by the name given in the proposals. It is a corporate body, like a company, which has a personality in law separate from the people who are members of it. An interim board of management has already been described. The number and type of members of the board of management will be as set out in the proposals. There must be four types of member: (a) parent members (who must form a majority); (b) staff members; (c) appointed members, one of whom must be a member nominated by the relevant denominational body (if appropriate); and (d) the headteacher.

21–15   There must be more parent members than there were on the former school board, but the same number of staff members. There must also be more appointed members than there

[7] Self-Governing Schools etc. (Scotland) Act 1989, s. 19 and Sched. 5.

were co-opted members on the former school board. As with school boards, parents elect the parent members and staff elect the staff members. Appointed members are, as the name suggests, appointed by the elected members of the board. Vacancies must be filled as soon as is reasonably practicable, but in any event within three months.[8]

Eligibility for Membership

Parents of pupils in attendance at the school may be parent **21–16** members. Members of the staff of the school may be staff members. Retiring members may be re-elected if they are still parents or members of staff.[9]

Disqualification from Membership

No one who is subject to a legal incapacity can be a member **21–17** of a board of management. If a person has been sequestrated or is bankrupt, or has been imprisoned for three months or more without the option of a fine for any offence, they also are disqualified. A further category of persons who are disqualified is those guilty of electoral practices contrary to Part III of the Representation of the People Act 1983.[10]

Term of Office

Board members serve for four years. When a board is first **21–18** constituted, however, half of the parent members serve for two years to ensure a rotation of members. If there is an odd number of parent members, then the number who initially

---

[8] Self-Governing Schools etc. (Scotland) Act 1989, s. 3(1)–(3).

[9] Self-Governing Schools etc. (Scotland) Act 1989, s. 3(1). A "parent" member is a person "elected to the board of management . . . by parents of pupils in attendance at the school from such parents". A "staff" member is "elected to the board of management . . . by members of staff of the school from such staff".

[10] Self-Governing Schools etc. (Scotland) Act 1989, s. 5.

serve only two years is the next whole number less than half. Failing agreement, the decision as to who resigns after two years is made by drawing lots. People who are elected to fill casual vacancies serve for the remainder of the term of office of the person whom they replaced.[11]

Proceedings of Boards of Management

21–19 Unless there is a rule of law governing the proceedings of boards of management, they are to regulate their own procedure. Their proceedings are not invalidated, even if there is a vacancy in the membership or a defect in the appointment or election of any member. Documents may be executed on behalf of a board by their being signed by one of the board members or by another person who has been authorised to do so, and sealed with the common seal of the board. Witnesses are not necessary.[12]

Powers and Duties of Boards of Management

21–20 The prime duties of a board of management are to manage the school and provide suitable and efficient school education in it. From the incorporation date, the board is empowered to receive from the authority any land, moveable property, liabilities and obligations transferred to it and also to acquire more land and property. It can dispose of land, but only with the prior written consent of the Secretary of State after he has consulted the authority. It should be noted that the term "dispose" is used, not "sell". It may be that a long lease would be covered by the term "dispose" and it would be prudent, therefore, to consult the Secretary of State even if something less than an outright sale were to be considered by the board.

21–21   Boards can also enter into contracts, raise and invest money, and accept outright gifts, or gifts in trust. They must also encourage the formation of parent/teacher or parents'

---

[11] Self-Governing Schools etc. (Scotland) Act 1989, s. 4.
[12] Self-Governing Schools etc. (Scotland) Act 1989, ss. 6 and 8.

associations and promote the use of the school premises and facilities by the community. In addition, they must provide adequate facilities for social, cultural and recreative activities and physical education and training, not only for their pupils, but also for the general public, if they so wish. There is also laid upon them a duty to have regard to the need to make improvements to the provision which the school makes for pupils with special educational needs. Liaison with parents is provided for by making boards of management report to them at least once a year about their activities in the same way as school boards. The rights of parents to call special meetings with school board representatives also applies in the same terms to boards of management.[13]

The Secretary of State may prescribe standards and general requirements to which boards must conform in carrying out their functions. Just as a complaint may be made to the Secretary of State if an authority fails to carry out its duties relating to the provision of education, the same rules apply to boards of management and intervention by the Secretary of State is equally possible. He may also require boards to provide him with reports and information about the schools. Boards can also require authorities to provide them with any administrative, professional, technical or other services which they provide to their own schools. Authorities may make reasonable charges for this but, in the event of dispute, the matter may be referred to the Secretary of State whose decision is final.[14]

21–22

Charging of Fees, etc.

The fact that a school is self-governing does not mean that it can behave like a private school and charge fees for providing school education. It cannot. However, it may charge fees for providing education or allowing its premises to be used for other purposes, for example to adults attending classes or for the hire of a hall. Just as it cannot charge pupils for school

21–23

---

[13] Self-Governing Schools etc. (Scotland) Act 1989, ss. 7 and 9.
[14] Self-Governing Schools etc. (Scotland) Act 1989, ss. 7, 9 and 34.

education, it must provide to pupils, free of charge, books, writing materials, paper, instruments, etc., indeed anything necessary for pupils to take full advantage of the education provided. One type of thing for which it can charge, but need not, is the provision of clothing for physical education or other activities for which special clothing is desirable.[15]

Staffing Matters

21-24 The views of the staff of a school which is seeking to achieve self-governing status have no bearing on the outcome. That is a matter decided by the ballot of parents and, thereafter, by the Secretary of State. If self-governing status is achieved, then the staff must follow the school and transfer to the employment of the board of management. This applies not only to teachers, but to anyone who works at the school or has even been designated to work at the school.

21-25 Although it is not thought that the matter has been tested, it is considered that the Transfer of Undertakings (Protection of Employment) Regulations 1981 would apply to such a transfer. Briefly, the effect of the regulations is that staff must transfer to the new employer on their existing terms and conditions of employment. Achieving self-governing status cannot be used as an excuse in itself, therefore, immediately to reduce pay or conditions although future re-organisations for certain reasons are not prohibited. An important feature of the regulations is the need to hold consultations with trades unions on what might broadly be described as the effect of the change of management. The time for this to begin would probably be when the decision of the Secretary of State granting self-governing status was announced. It is of great importance that the effects of the regulations are taken into account by school board and authority alike.

21-26 All that having been said, staff cannot refuse to transfer and opt to stay in the employment of the authority. Authorities might be tempted to transfer valuable employees from a school when the possibility of self-governing status looms, but there are pro-

---

[15] Self-Governing Schools etc. (Scotland) Act 1989, s. 11.

visions severely limiting their power over what are still their own staff. The basic rules governing transfer of staff are that anyone employed by the authority who works, or who has been assigned to work, solely at the school or who is designated by direction of the Secretary of State, transfers to the employment of the board of management as at the incorporation date. There are exceptions to this rule. Anyone whose contract terminates before the incorporation date does not transfer. Equally, anyone who was appointed or assigned to work solely at another school before that date or was withdrawn from work at the school before the incorporation date is exempt. The final category is school meals staff, but only if they provide meals for more than just the school, such as for meals on wheels. The contracts of employment of staff are then held to have been made between them and the board of management.

There are a number of limitations on the power of authorities **21–27** to manage the staff of schools where either a first resolution or a request to hold a ballot for the acquisition of self-governing status has been made and written notice of same received. Without the consent of the school board, authorities cannot do any of the following things:

(a) Appoint anyone to a vacancy of any kind which involves working solely at the school.

(b) Dismiss anyone from such a post.

(c) Alter, or agree to alter the terms and conditions of employment of any person working solely at the school unless the same alteration applies to all persons in such posts employed by them.

(d) Withdraw anyone from work at the school otherwise than by dismissing them.

Of course, first resolutions or a request for a ballot may not **21–28** always lead to self-governing status being achieved. If any of the following events happen, then the above restrictions do not apply:

(a) The council has not received notice of a second resolution within 46 days of having received notice of a first one.

(b) Where a ballot on the acquisition of self-governing status has been held with the result being a majority against the proposal and two weeks have passed without the Secretary of State having declared the ballot void.

(c) Proposals for the acquisition of self-governing status are either rejected by the Secretary of State or are withdrawn without a requirement to publish further ones.[16]

Effect on Proposed Changes to a School

21–29 There are some changes which cannot be made to a school without a consultation exercise being carried out with parents and other interested parties. Some changes even need the approval of the Secretary of State. For example, closing a school, changing its catchment area, etc., have to undergo such a procedure. Some of these changes are affected by a commencement of the opting-out procedure. So, where an authority has received written notice of either a first resolution for the acquisition of self-governing status or a request for a ballot, then any proposals by the authority to do the following things are suspended while the procedures for the acquisition of self-governing status are pending:
(a) Changing the site of the school.
(b) Changing the stages of education at a school (other than adding a nursery class).
(c) Making or changing arrangements for a special class at a school.
(d) Introducing, varying, or discontinuing arrangements for selective entry.
(e) Changing the admission criteria if based on the sex of the pupils.
(f) Changing from a denominational to a non-denominational school.[17]

Change in Characteristics of a Self-governing School

21–30 Schools do not exist in a vacuum. They should meet the educational needs of the part of the country which they serve. As indicated earlier, self-governing schools have their "characteristics" determined when they achieve self-governing status, but

[16] Self-Governing Schools etc. (Scotland) Act 1989, ss. 22 and 24.
[17] Self-Governing Schools (Suspension of Proposals) (Scotland) Order 1994.

there is no reason to expect that they should stay the same for ever. A means is allowed for the characteristics to be changed. After five years from the incorporation date, and earlier if the Secretary of State agrees, a board of management may, after consultation, resolve to seek a change in the characteristics and must then proceed to hold a ballot of parents on the matter. Consultation must first be held with the authority and the appropriate church or denominational body, if relevant. The board must tell the Secretary of State of the result of the ballot at once. If the result is in favour of change, the board must, within one month of the result, or such longer period as the Secretary of State may allow, publish the proposals for change and send a copy to the authority, Secretary of State and church or denominational body, if appropriate.

Any person may submit representations on the proposals to   **21–31** the Secretary of State with three months of publication. Publication involves the board placing an advertisement in a local newspaper saying that proposals for a change in characteristics have been sent to the Secretary of State and that representations may be made to him before the end of three months from the date of publication. It must also state where the proposals may be inspected. They must be available at the school and also, if the library authority (the council) agrees, at any public library within the area served by the school during normal working hours.

The Secretary of State may approve the proposals, having   **21–32** first considered the views of the authority on the effect of approval on their duty to secure the provision of adequate and efficient school education, the percentage of votes cast and such other matters as he considers appropriate. If he considers that he may reject the proposals, he must first consult the board on the possibility. If he considers that he may approve them with modifications, he must first consult both the board and the authority on the matter. In the event of a change in characteristics having the effect of a denominational school, which had previously been transferred to an authority, ceasing to be denominational, then compensation may be payable by the board to the denominational body.[18]

---

[18] Self-Governing Schools etc. (Scotland) Act 1989, ss. 30, 32 and Self-Governing Schools (Change in Characteristics) (Scotland) Regulations 1994.

Discontinuance of Self-governing School

21–33   Schools are occasionally closed by their owners, sometimes because parents cause all of the children to be educated elsewhere and sometimes because a new school is to replace the old one. A procedure for closure of self-governing schools is laid down.

21–34   A board has to resolve twice to discontinue its school, the second resolution being not less than 28 days and not more than 40 days after the first. Notice of the second resolution only must be given as soon as practicable, to the Secretary of State, the authority and the denominational body (if appropriate). Within six months of the second resolution, the board may publish its proposals and copy them to the Secretary of State, the authority and the church or denominational body, if appropriate. The published proposals must give the date of closure and be accompanied by a statement indicating whether or not any proposals for a new school have been published and explaining that anyone may submit representations to the Secretary of State on the matter within two months of the date of publication. The Secretary of State may approve or reject the proposals. If he proposes to approve them subject to modifications, he must first consult the board and the authority. In the event of the closure of a denominational school which had, before incorporation, been transferred to an authority, compensation may be payable to the denominational body by the board.

21–35   The Secretary of State cannot, at his own hand, close a school run by an authority. He does, however, have the power to close a self-governing school by withdrawing its funding. Again, a procedure for this is laid down. It begins by the Secretary of State serving notice on the board of his intention to withdraw funding as at a particular date having first consulted the board, the authority, the parents of the pupils and the denominational body, if appropriate. Somewhat curiously, the date must be at least seven years after the date of the giving of the notice. No doubt this lengthy period was set to allow all of the pupils attending a school to finish the stage of education which it supplied, but the effect on a school of a sentence postponed for so long can hardly be imagined.

21–36   There are exceptions to the seven-year rule. They are if the

Secretary of State is satisfied that the school is unsuitable to continue because of the small number of pupils attending and the relative cost involved, or because the board has failed substantially or persistently to comply or secure compliance with its legal duties. Not every failure will mean the closure of a school. The Secretary of State may specify what he thinks should be done to remedy the situation and give a time limit for specific action to be taken. Again, detailed procedures are laid down for this process and for this process and for action by him following a board's failure to comply with conditions. No consultation is needed in this case.

Where a school is to be discontinued or to cease to be 21–37 maintained by the Secretary of State he may make provision, by order, for the winding up of the school. The order will deal with such matters as the timetable for the winding up, arrangements for the dismissal of staff, ingathering of property, etc., and what is to become of the property. Interestingly, it may transfer the property to someone who wishes to open a new independent school in the one which is being wound up.[19]

Transfer of Property

To assist the transfer of property, the Secretary of State must 21–38 appoint a commissioner for school assets who has a number of powers to ensure that all that is done in this field is in accordance with the law. Authorities must reach agreement with him in writing as to all of the property, etc., which is to transfer and must give him such information on the subject as he may require.[20]

When a school acquires self-governing status, it is not only 21–39 the management of the school that passes from the authority to the board of management. The actual ownership of the school and the desks, books, etc., in it also transfer together with any liabilities and obligations relating to them. The same rule applies to anything which the school board has acquired. It too transfers with any obligations and liabilities relating to it.

[19] Self-Governing Schools etc. (Scotland) Act 1989, ss. 31, 32, 33, 50 and 52.
[20] Self-Governing Schools etc. (Scotland) Act 1989, s. 38 and Sched. 9.

Some property may have been held by the council for the use of more than one school. In such a case it transfers to the extent that it was used or held for the purpose of the self-governing school, that is to say that it has the same right to joint use after incorporation as it did before.

21–40   The exceptions to the rule in respect of property are hostels which remain in the ownership of the authority. Other things which do not transfer are:

(a) Any obligation by the authority to repay any loan incurred by the authority for the school.

(b) Any obligation to pay compensation to former staff for early retirement.

(c) Any obligation or liability under a contract of employment to a person not transferring to the employment of the board.

(d) Any liability of the authority where the cause of action arose before the incorporation date.

–41   The same rules on transfer apply to educational endowments which may be held by an authority for the purposes of a school. Endowments held for more than one school, including one which becomes self-governing, must continue to be administered by an authority as if the school was still in its control.

42   Once notice of a first resolution or of a request to hold a ballot has been received, an authority cannot change the use of school property (presumably with the intent of avoiding a transfer, although not necessarily) without the consent of the school board.[21] In addition, an authority cannot dispose of, or enter any agreement or unilateral obligation in respect of, any land or moveable property held wholly or partly for the purpose of the school unless: (i) the school board has first agreed, or (ii) it has not received timeous notice of a second resolution, or (iii) the ballot was not in favour of self-governing status and has not been declared void, or (iv) proposals for self-governing status have either been rejected or completely withdrawn.

If an authority has entered into an agreement or undertaken an obligation in breach of these conditions, the commissioner

---

[21] Self-Governing Schools etc. (Scotland) Act 1989, s. 36.

may, with the prior consent of the Secretary of State, serve a notice on the parties concerned which has the effect of breaking the agreement or obligation. This can only be done, however, if the agreement or obligation has not been actioned. The authority is taken to be the party which has breached the agreement or obligation.[22]

In addition, if the commissioner considers that an authority has wrongfully removed, transferred or is in the course of transferring property which he thinks should have gone to the self-governing school, he must refer the matter to the Secretary of State who will rule on the matter. The commissioner can also apply to the Court of Session for an order setting aside or varying a transfer or transaction involving property which should have passed to the self-governing school, subject to certain restrictions. **21–44**

Where the commissioner either cannot, or decides not to, raise such an action he may instead raise a different type of action, one which seeks to recover from the authority the value of the property wrongfully transferred and any expenses which he or the board have incurred because of it. He may raise the same type of action against an authority if it has simply removed property from a school after having received notice of a first resolution or a request for a ballot while the procedures for the acquisition of self-governing status are still ongoing.[23] **21–45**

---

[22] Self-Governing Schools etc. (Scotland) Act 1989, ss. 43 and 44.
[23] Self-Governing Schools etc. (Scotland) Act 1989, ss. 41, 42 and 46.

INTRODUCTION

The matters dealt with in the following appendices are not, with the exception of appeal committees, regulated by law. The ones relating to devolved school management, school development plans, appraisal of teachers and the Parents' Charter have been included because, although this work is concerned with the law relating to school education in Scotland, they are important innovations in the Scottish education system and readers may well be aware of their existence but not of their non-statutory nature.

Appeal committees have been included here because the subject is important in the context of several areas covered in the text.

APPRAISAL OF TEACHERS

In terms of section 70 of the Self-Governing Schools etc. **A1–01** (Scotland) Act 1989, the Secretary of State has power to make regulations requiring education authorities to appraise the performance of their teaching staff. He may also oblige authorities to make schemes for that purpose.

This power to make regulations has not been used, **A1–02** although it lies behind circular number 3/1991 issued by the Scottish Office Education Department, which invites authorities to prepare schemes for staff development and appraisal in accordance with the guidelines which it contains and to submit them to the Scottish Office. The guidelines are expected to be fully implemented in all schools by the beginning of the school session 1995/96.

The subject-matter which schemes are to cover are as **A1–03** follows:

(1) Management structures for staff development and appraisal.
(2) Arrangements for staff consultation and involvement.
(3) Identifying and prioritising staff development needs.
(4) Staff development programmes.
(5) The individual record of staff development.
(6) Appraisal of staff.
(7) Training appraisers and appraisees.
(8) Monitoring and evaluating staff development and appraisal arrangements and processes.
(9) Phasing the scheme in from 1992/93–1995/96.

DEVOLVED SCHOOL MANAGEMENT

A2–01 Education authorities are responsible for the management of public schools within their area and must carry out this responsibility within the framework of existing legislation. The Secretary of State, however, has substantial influence on education authorities through his ability to initiate new legislative provisions. It is as a result of this influence that the concept of "devolved school management" has been introduced generally to schools.

A2–02 Following consultation, the government decided that education authorities should bring forward administrative schemes of devolved management for all their primary, secondary and special schools.[1] These are schemes whereby substantial financial and management responsibility for each school is devolved to the school itself. The thinking behind this innovation is that the quality of decision-making will improve by giving schools greater flexibility and choice in deciding their own priorities and detailed arrangements in response to the needs of pupils. It is envisaged further that schools will be able to respond more quickly to changing needs within the school. There will also be greater accountability, with schools having a greater incentive to manage efficiently and to make more effective use of resources. In addition, it is believed that the morale of school staff will be raised as a result of the increased control and responsibility at school level for educational decisions.

A2–03 The overall effect is expected to be an improvement in the quality of education provided in schools throughout the country. Education authorities "will retain a strategic, enabling and supportive role while decisions at school level will be taken by

[1] SOED Circular 6/93: Devolved School Management Guidelines for Schemes, p. 5, para. 2.

headteachers, following consultation with their School Board where one exists."[2]

In introducing devolved school management, the Secretary A2–04
of State has issued guidelines only; he has not imposed a legal requirement on authorities to comply. He has, however, specified that schemes for devolved management should be firmly in place in all primary and secondary schools by April 1, 1996 and in all special schools by April 1, 1997.[3] He has also stated that the operation of the guidelines will be subject to review and that he "may wish to consider in due course whether there is a need for the arrangements to be supported by primary legislation, providing for a formal system of approval of schemes".[4]

So, while there is no obligation on authorities to introduce A2–05
devolved school management, the Secretary of State has made it clear that if it is not introduced voluntarily, he will consider making it compulsory by law. In fact, many authorities have prepared schemes in the hope that they will be better able to produce schemes more suited to the needs of their areas now, than if they had to comply with the requirements of later legislation.

The general principles on which schemes of devolved A2–06
school management are to be based are summarised as follows. Education authorities and all their schools should have clearly set out arrangements for the operation of their schemes and these will form part of their general policies. In drawing up the schemes, and at a later stage when assessing their effectiveness, authorities are to consult headteachers, staff and school boards. The latter should consult with parents to discover their views. Where there is no school board, then the parents of pupils at the school should be consulted by the authority. If appropriate, the views of other groups who make use of the school facilities should also be sought and taken into account.

Although there will be a single scheme which applies to all A2–07
of an authority's schools, there may be variations for different

---

[2] SOED Circular 6/93 p. 5, para. 2.
[3] SOED Circular 6/93, p. 8, para. 14.
[4] SOED Circular 6/93, p. 2, para. 6.

categories of school or for different geographical areas. The schemes are not required to cover nursery schools, but should take into account community use of schools and nursery departments within primary schools. The Scottish Office guidelines do not specify how financial resources are to be allocated to each school. Instead it is up to individual authorities to decide how this should be done. The aim must be to ensure a fair distribution of resources while recognising the particular needs of each school. Thus the scheme will indicate the authority's plans for special educational needs provision. Funds specifically allocated cannot thereafter be used for any other purpose. It is important that the scheme clearly sets out the allocation policy in order that all persons concerned can properly understand and assess it.

A2–08   In formulating the scheme, the aim should be to devolve to headteachers responsibility for decisions on all services and functions which relate solely or mainly to the individual school. Any functions already delegated to a school board under the School Boards (Scotland) Act 1988 cannot be included in the scheme. That functions are devolved under a scheme of devolved school management, however, does not mean that a school board may not seek delegation of some of those functions at some stage under the 1988 Act.[5]

A2–09   The scheme as drawn up will provide a structure for the operation of devolved management. The responsibility for decision taking will be devolved to the headteacher. In addition, however, provision will be made for the headteacher to consult the school board, if there is one, and to involve other school staff in exercising the responsibilities devolved. The headteacher must then take into account any views expressed by them. Although the school board must be consulted, particularly where it is proposed to spend considerable sums of money, the headteacher does not require the approval of the board. The existing statutory provision, however, whereby a headteacher requires the approval of the board for expenditure on books and teaching materials must be complied with.[6] In any other case where the headteacher

---

[5] SOED Circular 6/93, p. 5, para. 4 and p. 9, paras. 4 and 7. See also Chapter 20 on School Boards.
[6] School Boards (Scotland) Act 1988, s. 9.

and the school board disagree on proposed expenditure, the decision will rest with the headteacher. The school board could of course raise the matter with the education authority if it considered the matter to be serious. Where a school board does not exist, then the headteacher will be responsible for decision taking.

It is clearly important, in preparing the scheme, for the author-   A2–10
ity to identify all expenditure on school education. This will include spending at school level and costs incurred centrally by the authority. It is then necessary to define which areas of expenditure are to be excluded from the scheme and which would form part of the potential schools budget. The total education budget will include items which, according to the Scottish Office guidelines, need not be devolved to schools. Similarly, other areas of the overall budget will not relate to statutory school provision, for example community education. These will be excluded from the potential schools budget.

It is then up to the authority to identify the particular heads   A2–11
of expenditure relating to a particular school which are to be included in the scheme and to identify further the particular areas of spending on which decisions are to be taken by the headteacher in consultation with the school board. The Secretary of State expects schemes "to provide for significant devolved decision making on at least the following heads of expenditure: costs of staff wholly or mainly employed at the school, both teaching and non-teaching; furniture, fixtures and fittings; property-related costs; and supplies and services.[7]

The Secretary of State will not expect schemes to include   A2–12
devolved responsibility for budgets for capital programme expenditure nor the consequential loan charges arising in the revenue budget.[8] There are further areas of expenditure which need not be devolved to the school although they relate to the provision of services at school level and to individual pupils. They include: school meals and milk; bursaries, clothing and footwear grants; expenditure supported by central government grants; home to school transport; premature retirement costs; psychological and learning support services; and

---

[7] SOED Circular 6/93, p. 6, para. 6.
[8] SOED Circular 6/93, p. 6, para. 7.

upport for the integration of individual pupils with special educational needs and support for children with records of needs
provided by other services (for example health boards).

A2–13   Having reached a figure which can be defined as education
expenditure at school level, the authority must ensure that at
least 80 per cent is devolved to the control of headteachers
or delegated to school boards under the School Boards
(Scotland) Act.[9]

A2–14   To assist the practical operation of devolved management,
the scheme should provide for a degree of flexibility in dealing
with budgets. Thus it should allow for a degree of budget
carry-forward from one financial year to the next and set out
arrangements for dealing with surpluses and deficits. Headteachers should also be able to transfer funds between
budget heads both in-year and from one year to another.
Restrictions on these transfers should be within the authority's
guidelines and always have regard to the authority's discharge of its statutory duties and accountability.[10]

A2–15   Schemes of management are also expected to provide for
the involvement of the headteacher and school board in the
appointment of staff. The School Boards (Scotland) Act 1988
already regulates to an extent the appointment of headteachers, depute and assistant headteachers. Subject to this,
schemes should provide for delegating to the headteacher
the selection of other staff to be employed in the school, with
the possible involvement of the school board. Such provision
would, however, exclude persons working at the school but
employed by external contractors under CCT procedures.[11]

A2–16   Schemes should take account of the use of school premises
outwith school hours and the responsibility of the school
board in this regard. Any direction made by the education
authority in respect of such use must be included in the
scheme.[12]

[9] SOED Circular 6/93, p. 6, para. 8.
[10] SOED Circular 6/93, p. 7, paras. 9 and 10.
[11] SOED Circular 6/93, p. 7, para. 12.
[12] SOED Circular 6/93, p. 8, para. 13.

SCHOOL DEVELOPMENT PLANS

The Parents' Charter in Scotland 1995 in dealing with the **A3–01** assurance of quality of education in local schools, states: "By the start of the 1995–96 school year all schools will have to produce a school development plan setting out their educational plans and targets."[1] The plan is to be based on a three-year cycle with one year described in detail and the following two in outline. An annual review will continue the forward planning while reporting on the previous year's progress and evaluating actual performance in relation to targets set.

The purpose of the plan is to provide a framework for man- **A3–02** aging change for the benefit of pupils. It is intended to be a programme for improvement and positive action and should contain information related directly to learning and teaching. In drafting the plan, the headteacher should take account of the views of the staff and parents to whom the role of the development plan should be explained. A copy of the plan will be given to the school board, if one exists, and any parent may inspect it by approaching either the board or the school.

According to Scottish Office guidelines,[2] the school devel- **A3–03** opment plan should contain at least three sections as follows:

1. Aims

Aims are seen as fundamental to the development plan as **A3–04** subsequent assessment of performance must be related to the stated aims. This section of the plan should include a clear statement of the school's aims which will be readily under-

---

[1] *The Parents' Charter in Scotland 1995*, p. 14.
[2] "School Development Plans in Scotland 1994", Scottish Office Education Department.

stood by all interested parties, including parents, teachers and pupils. There should be a direct link between the aims, priorities and targets contained in the plan.

2. Audit

A3–05 This is very much the evaluation section. It should indicate how well the school is performing in the key areas of its work. The key areas include: first, for primary schools and special schools with primary age pupils, quality of the curriculum, quality of teaching and learning and pupil progress and attainment. These headings are appropriate for each class or stage level in the school. In addition, key overall areas would include management of staff, curriculum planning, available finance and resources, accommodation and "ethos" including relationships with pupils, parents, teachers and other school staff, and discipline and counselling.

A3–06 Secondly, for secondary schools and special schools with secondary age pupils, quality of courses, quality of learning and teaching, pupil progress and attainment, "ethos" – as defined above, curriculum planning, and accommodation and resources, including finance. These matters would be considered at departmental level. Again overall key areas would include management of staff, curriculum planning, available finance and resources, accommodation, guidance and "ethos".

A3–07 Having established the key areas relating to the school, the subsequent reviews of the development plan should contain an assessment of the quality of education in the school, identifying particular strengths and weaknesses. In this way, action can be taken to improve performance and quality. Examination results, where appropriate, and attendance rates are relevant indicators of performance and should be considered in a school audit.

A3–08 Although all key areas should be kept under review, there is no requirement to review every aspect each year. It is intended that schools should initially concentrate on areas which they consider require improvement, then move to other areas in order to cover all key areas in the course of the three-year cycle. As in the aims section, the views of parents, pupils, teachers and school boards should be taken into account in the audit section. Information obtained from them should be used in evaluating strengths and weaknesses of the school.

As well as identifying priority areas for development, the **A3–09** audit section will contain an evaluation of ongoing aspects of the school's work. These are sometimes referred to as "maintenance" areas. By reporting on these, the plan will show the balance between maintenance and future development.

3. Action

This section flows naturally from the previous two. Having **A3–10** identified the priorities to be addressed, the action section will specify what is to be done in the coming year. How many projects can be undertaken will depend on the circumstances of the particular school, for example the resources available and the level of staff training required. Each project in the action section should be specified as follows:

TARGETS which the project is designed to achieve – per- **A3–11** haps "to increase the attainment level of S4 pupils at Standard Grade", or "to develop functional writing within the 5–14 curriculum throughout the school", or "to agree and implement an anti-bullying policy".

CRITERIA FOR SUCCESS which are in effect the yardsticks **A3–12** by which the success or otherwise of the project will be measured. These criteria should be specified before the start of the project. Thus the criteria for the above targets might be stated as: "an increase of 5 per cent in the numbers of S4 pupils gaining a Standard Grade 1–3 award"; "clear evidence of functional writing in classrooms and progression in the variety of forms used"; "anti-bullying policy works well in the view of at least 80 per cent of staff, parents and pupils surveyed."

IMPLEMENTATION STRATEGIES or the methods by which **A3–13** the project will be carried out.

TIMESCALE for successful completion of the project. This **A3–14** should take account of all relevant factors including resources and staffing. It should be a realistic assessment of meeting targets within an acceptable period of time.

RESOURCES needed to complete the project successfully **A3–15** within the stated timescale. The necessary resources will vary with each project but are likely to include time, materials, finance and the need for staff development.

A3–16   EVALUATION PROCEDURES will provide a description of the ways by which evidence of the successful completion of each project will be obtained.

A3–17   Within the framework provided by the official guidelines, school development plans will contain projects which reflect priorities at both national and education authority level. They should, however, include as a matter of importance, the particular school's identified priorities.

A3–18   When the headteacher has, with the necessary consultation, finalised the plan and the education authority has agreed it, a copy should be provided for each member of the school board. Parents too should be informed of the plan and made aware that a copy is available for their inspection. In this way, information about the progress and priorities of the school can be made available to those concerned. Headteachers must decide how the information relating to the school development plan is to be presented to the school board alongside, or in parallel with, the annual report required by the School Boards (Scotland) Act 1988. Where no school board exists in relation to the school, consideration must be given to ways of obtaining the views of parents, perhaps through the parent/teachers association.

THE PARENTS' CHARTER IN SCOTLAND

In 1991, the Secretary of State for Scotland launched *The Parents' Charter in Scotland* which was produced under the general umbrella of the Government's *Citizen's Charter*. The booklet which was issued at the time was updated in 1995 and is available, free of charge, from the Scottish Office Education Department in Edinburgh. Its initial aim was to inform parents and to develop the partnership with schools and education authorities in line with *Citizen's Charter* principles. **A4–01**

The Charter sets out simply, but without detailed information, parents' rights as regards their children's education. It refers to the right to choose a school, to information, to a broad and balanced curriculum and the rights of children with learning difficulties. There is a section explaining what to do if things go wrong and another on quality of education in schools. The latter mentions the work of HM Inspectors whose independent inspections take account of parental views and whose reports identify the strengths and weaknesses of individual schools. The role of school boards is mentioned, as is devolved school management and the "opting out" procedure. **A4–02**

It should be noted, however, that the Charter is published by the Government as information only and does not itself have the force of law. Clearly, most aspects covered reflect the current legislation on education, but the document cannot be taken to be definitive in this respect. **A4–03**

APPENDIX 5

APPEAL COMMITTEES

A5–01   If a parent is not satisfied with an authority's decision on a placing request, with a decision to exclude a child from school, or decisions affecting his child's special educational needs, then he can appeal against such decision.[1]

A5–02   Although an appeal committee is established by the education authority, it is not a committee of the authority. It is an independent body under the supervision of the Scottish Committee of the Council on Tribunals.[2] It is made up of three, five or seven members nominated by the authority. The membership must comprise members of the authority (that is, elected councillors), or of the authority's education committee (which could include teachers' or religious representatives and co-opted members), and other people who are either: (a) parents of children of school age; (b) persons who in the opinion of the authority have experience in education; or (c) persons who in the opinion of the authority are acquainted with the educational conditions in the area of the authority. People who are employed in the education department of the authority may not be members.

A5–03   The people who are members of the education authority or the education committee may not outnumber the others by more than one. There is no rule to prevent the latter from outnumbering the former. The chairmanship may not be held by a member of the education committee, nor may any person who had a part in, or was even present at, discussions about the subject-matter of an appeal be a member of an appeal committee. Furthermore, there are others who may not be members of an appeal committee. They are teachers, pupils,

---

[1] See *Parents' Charter*, p. 12 and Education (Scotland) Act 1980, ss. 28(1), 28H and 63.

[2] Tribunals and Inquiries Act 1992, s. 1(1)(*a*).

parents of pupils or school board members at or of what is known as a "relevant school". A "relevant school" is one:

(1) Which a child, in respect of whom a placing request has been made, attends.
(2) Which is named in a placing request.
(3) Which an authority thinks a child, in respect of whom a placing request has been made, should attend.
(4) Which is a feeder school to a school in either (2) or (3).
(5) From which the pupil has been excluded.[3]

There are regulations which set out how hearings before **A5–04** appeal committees are conducted. Normally, they must be held within 28 days of a reference to the committee unless there are circumstances beyond the committee's control which prevent it. Dates may be varied if they are not convenient for the appellant.[4] At least 14 days' notice should be given of the time and place of the hearing. The appellant must also be told of his rights (a) to appear or be represented; (b) to have up to three friends including his representative with him; (c) to lodge written representations; and (d) to allow his case to rest solely on written representations.[5]

It may arise that more than one child may have had a pla- **A5–05** cing request refused for the same reason in respect of the same year of education at the same school or, in cases of exclusion from school, more than one child has been excluded at the same time for generally the same reasons. In such cases, appeals may be combined if the appeal committee so wishes, although appellants can address the committee with none of the others present if they so wish.[6]

Before the hearing begins properly, it would be good prac- **A5–06** tice for the chairman to introduce everyone present and to indicate in what capacity they are there. For example, the committee's clerk should be identified and the capacity in which each of the committee members attends.

The regulations lay down the procedure which must be fol- **A5–07**

---

[3] Education (Scotland) Act 1980, Sched. A1.
[4] The Education (Appeal Committee Procedures) (Scotland) Regulations 1982, regs. 7(1), (3) and (4).
[5] 1982 Regulations, regs. 8(1) and (2).
[6] 1982 Regulations, reg. 9.

lowed at the hearing itself although the appeal committee can vary it on cause shown. The education authority presents its case first. The appellant may then ask questions. Then the appellant presents his case and the education authority may ask questions. When that has been done, the authority sums up its case. The last word lies with the appellant who then sums up.[7] Although the regulations do not provide for it, members of the committee may, it is thought properly, ask questions of either side during the course of the appeal, e.g. to clarify points that have been made. Either side may call witnesses to speak to points they wish to make.[8] The committee does not have to give its decision and the reasons for it on the day of the hearing although it must do so in writing within 14 days. If it does not intend to give its decision in writing with reasons at the end of the hearing, the chairman must tell the parties that before the hearing ends.[9] Each member of the committee must vote on a decision.[10]

A5–08   If the decision is against the appellant, he must be informed of his right of appeal to the sheriff. The education authority has no right of appeal.[11]

[7] 1982 Regulations, reg. 11(2).
[8] 1982 Regulations, reg. 11(3).
[9] 1982 Regulations, reg. 14(1) and (2).
[10] 1982 Regulations, reg. 13(5).
[11] 1982 Regulations, reg. 14(2).

INDEX